To Mom.
Happy Birthday '92

Love
Tracy

the book of Women

300 Notable Women History Passed By

Lynne Griffin & Kelly McCann

Illustrations: Joanna Hudgens

Published by Bob Adams, Inc.
260 Center Street, Holbrook, MA 02343

ISBN: 1-55850-106-1

Printed in the United States of America

A   B   C   D   E   F   G   H   I   J

COVER PAINTING: Leonid Mysakov (Irmeli Holmberg)

ACKNOWLEDGMENTS

This book would not be complete if we neglected to thank the following people and institutions who helped make it possible: Mrs. Duncan Todd Bates of Scituate, Massachusetts; the public libraries of Brookline and Boston, Massachusetts; Steve Brown; Lucy Shelton Caswell of the Ohio State University Cartoon, Graphic, and Photographic Arts Research Library; Christopher Ciaschini; The Embassy of the Hellenic Republic of Greece; Lisa Fisher; Jody Habayeb of the *Fort Wayne News-Sentinel*; Peter Gouck; Catherine Hughes of the International Museum Theatre Alliance; Wayne Jackson; Diana James; Jeff Marcus of Job-Link; Nancy McGovern; Dr. Carol Meyers, Director of the Department of Women's Studies at Duke University; the staff of the National Baseball Hall of Fame; the staff of the National Council of Jewish Women; Gigi Ranno; the Scituate (Massachusetts) Historical Society; Gloria Steinem; Brandon Toropov; and Dr. Evan Harris Walker of the U.S. Army Ballistic Research Laboratory.

A special note of thanks goes to the Daughters of the American Revolution, who provided invaluable source material on the following women of their organization who appear in this book: Kate Waller Barrett; Caroline Harrison; Patty Smith Hill; Mildred Hill; Jessica M. Hill; Julia Ward Howe; Belle Reynolds; and Ruth Bryan Owen Rohde.

DEDICATION

INTRODUCTION

Item: In 1897, Lena Jordan turned the first triple somersault on the flying trapeze in circus history. Until recently, record books listed Ernest Clarke, who managed the triple in 1909, as the first to perform the feat. Up until the mid-Seventies, the *Guinness Book of World Records*, which had perpetuated the original error for years, listed Jordan and Clarke side-by-side, noting the respective dates—but declining the opportunity to honor Jordan with a solo listing for her accomplishment.

Item: A well known volume on American history in our local library features nearly six hundred index listings at the rear of the book. Of these, there are twelve listings naming women.

Item: Of the nearly seven thousand entries in a recent bestseller whose cover boasts of summarizing "what every American needs to know," a total of sixty-nine women are referenced.

Item: An analysis of a recent front page of *The Wall Street Journal* revealed that male newsmakers identified by name outnumbered their female counterparts by almost eight to one.

❑   ❑   ❑

Women often seem to vanish into thin air.

Books, magazines, newspapers, and the innumerable other sources that shape our sense of popular history tend, even today, to focus more on the opinions, objectives, and accomplishments of men than on those of women. The result is a skewed world view that leaves women and fair-minded men to wonder when, if ever, we will be able to boast of an objective approach to the women who have shaped and continue to shape our world.

We don't know when that will take place, and we certainly don't expect to solve the problem overnight. We do know that the "invisibility problem" does not arise from an absence of women whose stories are worth hearing. This book is the proof.

From penning the world's first novel to walking a tightrope across a roaring waterfall; from printing the first copies of the Declaration of Independence to setting the strategy behind the Union's Tennessee campaign in the Civil War; from claiming (often illegally!) the right to vote to controlling the White House of a stricken chief executive, women's accomplishments have been underplayed, selectively rewritten, and just plain ignored for far too long.

We began this book with the idea that most open-minded people felt in their bones that there was probably more to the story of female achievement than they knew or had been told. We also felt strongly that this state of affairs was likely to bother people, because it bothered us. We wanted to know: Where was the rest of the story? Who were some of the women who had been passed over? We set out to answer that for ourselves.

❑   ❑   ❑

Is there a danger in focusing "only on women" when our complaint is with those who focused "only on men"? This is a fair question; our answer is that the risk is worth taking.

For one thing, there are simply too many fascinating women to ignore. Who would have guessed that the first person of either sex to go over Niagara Falls in a barrel and live was a forty-three year old female schoolteacher who couldn't swim? For another thing, there are vast gaps to be filled. If our research for this project had led us to believe that there really were, for instance, only twelve women of importance in American history, we might have attacked the job differently. As it stands, however, we feel compelled to focus intensely on at least some of the undone work—even if that means repeating, to a degree, the error of sex-based exclusion. Our attempt is to nudge the ship back on course after many leagues of misdirected travel.

Make no mistake. *The Book of Women* is not a "women's view of history." It is an attempt to gather some important—and not widely known—accounts of remarkable women through the centuries. We have sought to collect and present these accounts in an interesting manner, and we have tried to speak to a large and growing audience composed primarily of two groups. The first: those who may have grown up with no real reason to believe that women could have (up until a few years ago, at least) played leading roles in much of anything, but who are close to someone who knows otherwise. The second: those who feel that women *must* have accomplished more, sought more, lived more than the record seemed to indicate—but were often hard put to provide specifics.

We feel it's fair to say that one major reason for the "invisibility problem"—past and present—has been that those composing our histories have, by and large, been males. In the end, of course, the stories must speak for themselves, and we feel they do. The women whose accomplishments, trials, betrayals, and long-range hopes lie within these covers are their own justification.

❑   ❑   ❑

A word is in order on the way we went about choosing the women in this book.

Ann Richards, the governor of Texas, recently told an interviewer that her role model as a young girl was Wonder Woman. We can't help wondering whether her selection of a comic book superhero was as much a matter of necessity as reach-for-the-stars personal empowerment. How many women before Richards had conquered the rough-and-tumble circus of confrontation and personal dominance that is Texas politics? What flesh-and-blood woman *could* she have chosen?

By and large, growing up female means growing up without famous, larger-than-life females to emulate. That may be less true today than it was a few decades ago—thanks in no small measure to women like Ann Richards—but it is still a fact of life for most girls and women. One of the main motivators for us in working on this book was the idea that we were on a mission. We were in search of the great heroines so long denied to us.

Before we began the search, however, we had to stop to consider the kinds of women who often *have* won wide recognition in our popular history. These, we found, typically included heroic, self-sacrificing angels (Florence Nightingale, Clara Barton), sex-as-weapon temptresses (Cleopatra, Mata Hari), and companions to famous male figures (Dolley Madison, Martha Washington). To be sure, there were some notable exceptions, but the general outlines of the picture were clear.

A. *Martyrs.* Women could serve as pseudo-divine healers in time of disaster, impossibly pure saints removed from the petty personal concerns of the real world, saviors who could always be counted on to put their own interests in the background for the good of others.

B. *Whores.* Women could use sex to get ahead.

C. *Wives.* Women could stand by their man.

Was that all? Who, we found ourselves wondering, were the inventors? The mathematicians? The adventurers? The founders of nations? Who, for that matter, were the criminals and the scam artists? Was the lack of public knowledge of female historical figures in such areas due to the fact that there simply had been no such women? We didn't think so. And it didn't take us long to confirm our suspicions. It remains to be seen whether Margaret Knight, Amalie Noether, Dora Keen, Himiko, Molly Frith, or Therese Humbert will become household names. But for the young women now coming of age, we feel that having their stories in a single volume is an improvement and then some over the status quo.

Who *didn't* merit consideration for inclusion in the book? This was one of the more difficult questions. After a good deal of reflection and discussion, we decided that, since the main thrust of the book was to shed light on women whose stories had yet to be widely circulated, we would pass over any well known sports, literary, and entertainment figures—even if they boasted significant accomplishments outside their primary discipline. Using the same logic, we omitted, with some reluctance, such pioneering activists as Susan B. Anthony and Carry Nation. Our book's aim, then, was not to tell of the most important women in popular history, but to tell of some of the most unjustly ignored.

Another temptation we resisted was to turn the book into an almanac of the accomplishments of the female sex. As fascinating as it might have been to concern ourselves solely with such matters as the identity of the first woman to cross the Atlantic, win an Olympic medal, or write a *New York Times* bestseller, we ultimately decided that this slant offered silent complicity with the notion that men always did worthwhile things first.

Having abandoned the almanac approach, we nevertheless found that there were a number of "firsts" where credit had simply been denied to women—credit for very important work indeed. In these instances, we (and, no doubt, you) had been led to believe as schoolchildren that males had, on their own, accomplished certain things that now looked to have been done by or in partnership with women. And these were not minor achievements: the discovery of the "Missing Link," for one; the development of the Theory of Relativity, for another.

Even with such after-the-fact success stories to reckon with, we did not confine ourselves to telling the stories of laudable women. That, too, was a trap we felt obliged to avoid. We considered the notion that a woman is unable, by nature, to commit forgery, murder another person, or counterfeit money to be as oppressive as the notion that she is "meant" to devote her life to childrearing or housekeeping. (The principle that readers don't want to hear about such antisocial women, which still seems to underlie much male thinking in this area, struck us as similarly short-sighted.)

Nor, by any means, are all the women profiled here idealists or pioneers. Many had to compromise and adopt halfway measures to remain viable participants in their chosen fields. Then as now, this was a reality of female life that we felt should be reflected in the text. Our history—as both women and human beings—is not merely a series of iconoclasts and daring challengers; those who held back, took what they could win at the moment, and sought more another day had (and have) their part to play.

We should note, too, that there were certain built-in disadvantages to our project. The most notable was the problem of the anonymous champion. A woman who, over time, summons up vast reserves of courage, endurance, and ingenuity to win a place of high honor in a male-dominated field stands out; a woman whose accomplishments lie in subtle, incremental, and unattributed accomplishments over a comparable period of years often does not. We have no doubt that there are scores of such women whose quiet efforts and long-term victories would merit a place in this volume—but we have no way of knowing who they are or were. We have tried to compensate for this by featuring a number of stories of women for whom the main accomplishment was not flamboyant levels of worldly success, but the act of steadily and implacably maintaining a sense of validity and personal identity despite adversity. This, too, is a battle, and those who wage it successfully should be celebrated.

Finally, our list is, almost by definition, not an exhaustive one. We could paraphrase the New Testament by pointing out that if the stories of all the women one *should* have heard of were committed to paper, the whole world would not be sufficient to house the volumes that would be written. There are hundreds, thousands of women whose stories are waiting to be told. We could not possibly address even a significant portion of them here. But *The Book of Women* is one book, a book that tells some of their stories, a book that is meant not for scholars and lecturers and researchers but for open-minded people of both sexes—and that is, we hope, enough for a start.

❑   ❑   ❑

There is a myth that "the women's movement" is a twentieth-century phenomenon. A glance through these pages should dispel that idea quickly enough. In countless ways, generations of women have been knocking over walls and negotiating obstacles wherever they found them for a good many centuries now. They will continue to do so, even though, for some reason, their efforts may not win the immediate notice they seem to warrant. The pattern, however, is unmistakable: When they are denied fundamental equality, remarkable women will find ways to make their lives work, no matter what.

No. The women's movement—by whatever name it is called—is not a recent development. It is male awareness of it that is new. It follows that this book is as relevant for men as for women . . . and, paradoxically, perhaps most relevant to those men who wonder why it was written. To be sure, they may not read it. But there is nothing to stop people from relating its stories to them at key points of the conversation!

We, like you, live in a cynical age, but we came away from our time with *these* remarkable women with a powerful feeling of optimism: a sense that anything, in the end, is possible. The varied and compelling stories—heroic and devious, daring and cautious, quiet and bold—offer inspiring responses to restrictions, obstacles, and stereotypes. They are, if nothing else, impossible to ignore. They reaffirm to us that there is really no way for anyone to make a woman vanish. All one can do is close one's eyes. And no one can do that forever.

—*L.G.*
—*K.M.*

TABLE OF CONTENTS

THE BOOK
OF WOMEN

ALLIES ABANDONED

Women Who Made
Male Success Stories Possible . . .
and Never Shared the Glory

Catherine Lidfield Greene

Eli Whitney's cotton gin was recognized as the single most important American invention to date shortly after he acquired a patent for it in 1793. It revolutionized American agriculture and made Whitney a legend. However, it wasn't his idea. Catherine Greene, mistress of a Georgia plantation, was the first to theorize a machine capable of stripping seeds from balls of cotton. Whitney was a guest at Greene's home; she supported him for six months and added final touches to the model he eventually made famous. Although Whitney never became a rich man as a result of his invention, he did become famous, which is more than can be said of Greene. She proposed the idea, financed it, and made final alterations on it; nevertheless, it was under Whitney's name that the cotton gin was registered.

Elizabeth Jane Wimmer

The history books tell us that John Sutter and James Marshall were the ones who located gold in January of 1848 at Sutter's Mill in Coloma, California. What they don't tell us is that Elizabeth Wimmer, who ran a local boarding house, had been insisting that there was gold in the region for weeks beforehand. Wimmer, who had grown up near the gold mines of Georgia, was the one who first positively identified the strange rock Marshall found by placing it in a tub of soap suds. ("If it comes out bright," she explained to Marshall, "it is gold.") Marshall rushed to tell Sutter of his discovery, and the great gold rush was on. Wimmer's role—and her chance to clean up figuratively as well as literally—was quickly forgotten.

Sylvia Beach

Beach was the owner of the small Paris bookstore, Shakespeare & Co.; in 1922, she published the first edition of James Joyce's *Ulysses*. Beach was instrumental in getting the controversial book into print (it had been banned from publication in Britain), proofread the galleys, and helped to smuggle the novel into Canada and the United States. She

SYLVIA BEACH

didn't bother to write up a contract with the author. Although she printed eleven editions of the book, she received no share of the massive profits that came Joyce's way when the U.S. Supreme Court, by declaring the work not to be obscene, opened the door for a mainstream release. Her bookshop closed in 1941 after Beach nearly went bankrupt.

BEHIND THE SCENES
Remarkable Companions of
Male Historical Figures

Khadijah
Khadijah was the first wife of the prophet Mohammed, founder of Islam. Records indicate that she was a successful merchant and approximately fifteen years older than her twenty-five-year-old fiancé when the two married. She supported Mohammed financially after his historic first vision in 610 A.D., and was an enthusiastic proponent of his mission.

Hanna Penn
Although William Penn is known as Pennsylvania's founder, it was his second wife, Hanna, who kept the colony from falling back into British hands. Plagued by bad business decisions, Penn was nearly bankrupt and his colony was in danger of being repossessed by the British Crown when he suffered a massive stroke in 1712. As a woman, Hanna could not legally take over the affairs of her husband's colony, but she masterfully utilized her contacts in the British government to gain that privilege. Hanna signed her husband's name to colonial documents, appointed a governor for the colony, and deftly managed pressures to disband the colony from both the Crown and leaders in Pennsylvania. She was also successful in settling a border dispute with Maryland in her colony's favor. By keeping the British away from Penn's holdings, she secured colonists fundamental rights such as freedom of religion and trial by jury. These rights were to become the cornerstones of the American Constitution.

Constanze Mozart

Having suffered through miserable poverty in the final years of the legendary composer's life, Constanze showed considerable inventiveness and business sense in "resurrecting" her husband's compositions. She arranged for public performances of his works, coordinated the sale of Mozart's manuscripts to the publisher André, and saw the first substantive biography of the composer through to publication in 1828. She played an important part in the public's reappraisal of her husband, who, despite his genius, never achieved in life the level of success his work merited.

CONSTANZE MOZART

Caroline Harrison

When her husband Benjamin Harrison was inaugurated as President in 1889, Caroline became First Lady of the land. Early in her husband's administration, she was asked to assist in fundraising efforts for a new medical school: Johns Hopkins. She agreed to take on the task only after negotiating a pledge from the school to admit women and men on an equal basis. So it was that Harrison, considered one of the most domestically oriented of all First Ladies, helped further the cause of equal opportunity.

Czarina Maria Fyodorovna

Czar Alexander III had decreed that a certain criminal was to be exiled to Siberia, a fate that meant sure death. Alexander had scrawled at the bottom of the man's warrant the following sentence: "Pardon impossible, to be sent to Siberia." The Czarina apparently viewed the case more leniently, and altered the punctuation: "Pardon, impossible to be sent to Siberia." The man was freed.

"BLASPHEMY!"
Women Whose Ideas Raised Eyebrows and Blood Pressures

Lucy Stone

Stone, pioneering activist and editor of the influential suffragist newspaper the *Woman's Journal*, carried her egalitarian convictions into her personal life. She composed a then unheard-of document she called a marriage contract with her future husband, Henry Blackwell, in which the pair defined themselves as equals. She then had the audacity to refer to herself as "Mrs. Stone" after marriage. Those women who followed her example were blithely referred to as "Lucy Stoners."

Anne Josephe Theroigne De Mericourt

This fiery singer and courtesan dressed up as an Amazon to storm the Bastille during the French Revolution; she was also the leader of the Women's March on Versailles in October of 1789. De Mericourt was an ardent feminist who was years, if not centuries, ahead of her time; she was also one of the era's most radical antimonarchists, advocating wholesale war against all sitting European monarchs. She became caught up in partisan postrevolutionary conflicts and quickly fell out of favor with the public; her untempered feminism probably didn't help matters much. After being physically attacked by a mob in 1793, she underwent a personal collapse that culminated in her internment in an insane asylum one year later. There she spent the final two decades of her life.

Fanny Wright

How radical is radical? In the U.S. in 1828, Fanny Wright was about as far on the fringe as you could get: she spoke out against slavery, advocated the right of individuals of both sexes to choose their sexual partners outside of the legal bounds of marriage, and suggested that intermarriage could eventually solve the country's race problem. This was more than the newspaper writers of the day could stand: Wright was branded by apoplectic male observers as a "blasphemer," a "preacher of licentiousness," and a promoter of "vice and sensuality in its most loathsome form."

LUCY STONE

TO BOLDLY GO WHERE NO MAN OR WOMAN . . .
Great Female Adventurers

"Petit Jean"

Her true name will probably never be known; what we do know about this intrepid woman is that she was betrothed to a French nobleman by the name of Chavet and wanted desperately to accompany him on his expedition to the New World in the early 1800s. He did not believe she could live the rugged life in the Americas. She disagreed, disguised herself as a boy (not even Chavet recognized her) and served ably as cabin boy for the long voyage. She was an important member of the crew during the grueling summer-long exploratory mission, but she succumbed to a sudden fever before the group could return to France. She confessed her true identity and asked to be buried on one of the mountaintops near present-day Morrilton, Arkansas. Chavet went back to Paris without the woman he loved.

Osa Johnson

Johnson, a wildlife photographer, conducted a number of pioneering forays into Africa and Polynesia between 1910 and 1937 that make modern clichés associated with early jungle expeditions look tame by comparison. During one harrowing encounter in the South Seas, she and her traveling companion were actually captured by a group of quite genuine cannibals. The natives were eventually won over by her hastily developed photographs of tribe members.

Dora Keen

Her successful 1912 expedition to reach the peak of Alaska's 13,690-foot Mount Blackburn was the first to succeed without Swiss guides, the first to feature a prolonged night ascent, and the first to reach its goal by means of an avalanche-swept southeast face. She saw her company through snowstorms, avalanches, and sub-zero temperatures; one particularly tough storm forced the eight-person, nine-dog team to retreat to a cave for thirteen days.

OSA JOHNSON

BREAKING NEW GROUND
Forerunners in Women's Rights

Margaret Brent

This remarkable Colonial landowner, in constant legal dispute with bewildered men, may have been the first advocate for women's rights in America. How she managed to achieve a position of high status in Maryland is not entirely certain; her career, unparalleled in the era, seems to have taken off when she was named executor of the will of the governor of the colony. Brent later bought land with enthusiasm and appeared in court with her many male adversaries 124 times in eight years. She always represented herself, and she won every case. Brent made a landmark plea on January 21, 1647, when she argued that she should be granted two votes in the colonial assembly: one as a landowner and the other as an attorney. The ingenious request was denied—but it made Brent the first American suffragist.

Harriot K. Hunt

Hunt, who had studied medicine in England, practiced as an extremely capable doctor in Boston for forty years despite the best efforts of the all-male medical establishment to pretend she did not exist. She could not win entrance to medical lectures or attain formal degrees, but she could—and did—earn a great deal of money. Hunt lodged formal protests against the taxes levied on her sizable income, arguing that taxing her was inappropriate unless she was granted a vote in town affairs. Her protests were always ignored. And they were always reissued by the doctor each year at tax-collection time.

Abby and Julia Smith

In 1869, these Glastonbury, Connecticut, sisters—both in their seventies—refused to pay their taxes unless granted the right to vote in town meetings. They were decades ahead of the prevailing attitudes of the nation (women would not win the right to vote nationwide until 1920), and authorities quickly seized their livestock. The pair bought their cows back twice—and twice refused to pay. The animals were reseized each time. The ongoing conflict brought the sisters international publicity, although they did not win the votes they had sought.

ALICE PAUL

Alice Paul

This trailblazing activist brought English suffragist techniques back to her native America; she was also the author of the first equal rights amendment. The 1923 "Lucretia Mott" amendment was never passed by Congress. In the 1970s, Paul—now an elderly woman—supported the later Equal Rights Amendment just as unhesitatingly. That amendment did make it to the state legislatures, but it fell a handful of states short of adoption. Paul died in 1977 and never saw her ideas ratified into the United States Constitution. The wait continues.

BREAKTHROUGH!
Winning Medical Science's Battles

Louise Pearce
Dr. Pearce was one of the main figures in the development of the drug tryparsamide, which, when introduced on a wide scale, wiped out an epidemic of the deadly disease known as African sleeping sickness. She and her colleagues were awarded the Order of the Crown of Belgium, the King Leopold II Prize, and the Royal Order of the Lion for their work.

Grace Leidy and Hattie Alexander
In 1950, this team developed techniques making it possible to produce hereditary changes in *Hemophilus influenzae*, responsible for certain problematic strains of bacterial meningitis. Working on her own in 1939, Alexander had been the first person to bring about a successful treatment of infants afflicted with influenzal meningitis, which until then had been fatal.

Lady Mary Montagu
Although it was Edward Jenner who perfected the vaccine method against smallpox, its first Western advocate was Lady Mary Montagu, herself a victim of the disease. In 1715, she suffered an infection that left her disfigured for life; the following year, while accompanying her husband on a trip to Turkey (he was the British Ambassador), she noticed that Turkish doctors could scratch a healthy person with an infected needle and produce a mild case of the disease that would leave the sufferer immune to serious bouts. She insisted that doctors perform the proce-

dure on her four-year-old son, and later introduced the approach to England. Lady Montagu was credited with saving thousands of British lives.

Helen Brooke Taussig

"Blue babies"—those who come into the world processing oxygen inefficiently due to a constriction in a key artery between the heart and lungs—are now much more likely to live since the introduction of the Blalock-Taussig operation in 1945. Dr. Alfred Blalock was the doctor who perfected the technique's surgical execution; the initial idea—which involves creating a new vessel—was Dr. Taussig's. An immensely influential procedure,

HELEN BROOKE TAUSSIG

Blalock-Taussig laid the groundwork for most of today's cardiac surgery, which was once considered to be so dangerous that it was very rarely attempted. Dr. Taussig's role in the development of this landmark operation, which has saved untold thousands of babies' lives, earned her the Medal of Freedom, the highest civilian honor an American President can bestow.

BY ANY MEANS NECESSARY
Women Who Made Themselves Heard

Mary Jackson

In 1863, amid the economic chaos of the war-torn Confederacy, Jackson organized a group of Richmond, Virginia, wives and mothers demanding food at affordable prices. There were numerous bread riots in the South during this time, but Jackson's was notable in its organization (over one thousand women rallied with her) and its location (the Confederate capitol). Jackson herself, armed with a Bowie knife and a six-gun, led the desperate women on a rampage through downtown Richmond that marked the most significant domestic crisis to face beleaguered Confederate president Jefferson Davis. He tried to calm the women with rhetoric and the little cash he had in his own pockets, but they would not disperse. Finally, the city battalion was called in to quell the uprising.

Lucy Burns

Together with legendary activist Alice Paul, Burns organized a massive woman suffrage demonstration for March 3, 1913, in Washington D.C. It was probably not complete coincidence that that was also the date on which Woodrow Wilson was to be inaugurated as President of the United States. When Wilson showed up at the Capitol, he found that his greeters had left to see the big parade. The crowd of over five thousand marchers demanding a constitutional amendment granting women the right to vote made quite a splash as they elbowed their way down crowded Pennsylvania Avenue. (The amendment they sought was passed and ratified before Wilson left office.)

Emmaline, Christabel, and Sylvia Pankhurst

Emmaline and her two daughters Christabel and Sylvia founded the Women's Social and Political Union (WSPU) in 1903. Their organization's focus was on radical forms of direct action as a method to promote women's suffrage. Direct they were: the group's members marched on Parliament, chained themselves to railings, and in general looked around for the most interesting and appropriate ways to get themselves arrested. It all made news. Emmaline, in particular, had a huge impact on the dawning suffrage movement in the United States. Her many prison hunger strikes and other forms of protest received much media attention

FANNIE LOU HAMER

and were difficult to ignore; the British establishment nevertheless made a valiant effort. Emmaline died on June 14, 1928, shortly after passage of England's second Representation of the People Act, which granted equal suffrage to men and women.

Fannie Lou Hamer

One of the premier strategists of the civil rights movement, Hamer helped lead the historic Freedom Democratic Party challenge against the all-white Mississippi delegation at the 1964 Democratic National Convention. Though her delegation made headlines, it was brushed aside by a cautious Lyndon Johnson. Hamer's group won partial representation in 1968, and—finally—was acknowledged as the sole legitimate Mississippi representatives at the 1972 convention.

BY THE BOOK
Women Who Broke New Ground in Literature

Enheduanna
This Sumerian writer and high priestess, who lived circa 2000 B.C., was more than the first recorded female poet. She is believed by some scholars to be the author of the first attributed literary effort in history. Her verses to the moon God Inanna were reverenced for centuries.

Lady Murasaki Shikibu
This Japanese noblewoman, who was born in 970 and died in 1004, is among the very earliest great literary figures of any culture. She wrote *The Tale of Genji*, the earliest novel on record. The work, which concerns itself with adventure and romance in the court of eleventh-century Japanese royalty, is considered a masterpiece by many critics.

Hrosvitha
A tenth-century nun in the German convent at Gandersheim, Hrosvitha composed a wide variety of poems and comedies for the entertainment and instruction of her fellow sisters. Her work may have been the basis for some of the miracle plays that were performed in the early stages of the European theatre's development.

Christine de Pisan
This fourteenth-century French woman is believed to be the first European woman to make a living as a writer. After her husband died in the early 1390s, she com-

posed a series of ballads and stories that won favor in court circles. An advocate of female emancipation, Pisan was probably the first woman who could be called a feminist writer.

Anne Bradstreet

Bradstreet was the first published poet in American history. She abandoned a life of nobility in England to settle with her husband in Massachusetts sometime before 1644. Her poems were first published in London in 1650 in a collection entitled *The Tenth Muse Lately Sprung Up in America*. A later collection, *Several Poems Compiled with Great Variety (of) Wit and Learning*, was published posthumously.

ANNE BRADSTREET

Her verses, composed while Bradstreet attended to her family of ten, show a fascinating insight on Puritan life in the colony; they concern themselves with Bradstreet's love for her husband, her anguish at the death of her children, her fear of death in childbirth, and the business of reassembling life in the face of hardship.

CIVIL WAR HEROINES
Women Who Made a Difference in America's Bloodiest War

Mary Bickerdyke

Bickerdyke was a one-woman whirlwind whose sole aim during the Civil War was to more efficiently care for wounded Union soldiers, no matter what. If improving the level of care meant scrubbing up after filthy, incompetent doctors, then she would scrub every surface in sight. If improving the level of care meant antagonizing the hospital staff by threatening to report drunken physicians, then she would antagonize them. If improving the level of care meant ordering a staff member who had illegally appropriated garments meant for the wounded to strip the clothes off, then she would order him to strip! Bickerdyke stepped on a lot of male toes, but she won most of her fights. One ruffled male appealed to General William Tecumseh Sherman to take action against her, but was disappointed by the reply he received: "Well, I can do nothing for you; she outranks me."

Mary Livermore

Hearing of desperately bad conditions in Union camps, Livermore, the wife of a Chicago minister, put her children under the watchful eye of her housekeeper and started full-time work founding chapters of the United States Sanitary Commission. She initiated over three thousand of the local organizations in the Midwest, and is given credit for saving Grant's troops at Vicksburg from succumbing to an epidemic of scurvy. Livermore did it by supplying such massive amounts of fresh produce to the Union lines that a contemporary observer noted that "a line of vegetables connect(s) Chicago and Vicksburg."

Sally Tompkins

Because the South lacked the North's tremendous resources and railroad capacity, private hospitals had to do the job of the Union side's Sanitary Commission. In Sally Tompkins's facility, 1,260 of 1,333 wounded Confederate soldiers survived, a recovery level no other facility on either side of the Mason-Dixon line would match during the war. Tompkins managed her Richmond, Virginia, facility with a staff of seven—and that figure included Tompkins herself.

ANNIE WITTENMEYER

Mehitable Ellis "Auntie" Woods

Woods was so devoted to the Union soldiers from her home state of Iowa that she secured her own commissary wagon and personally made supply runs to the front lines—unaccompanied. She was often questioned by military officials about her authorization, but she routinely passed through by simply answering that she was going "to see my sons, all of whom are in the army." She made thirteen perilous trips in all.

Annie Wittenmeyer

Wittenmeyer, too, financed her own trips to the front, where she brought over $130,000 worth of supplies. When she saw her own brother being provided with substandard infirmary rations (coffee, rancid bacon, and bread), she established her Special Diet Kitchens to bolster the often inedible army fare offered to wounded and dying Union soldiers.

CLANDESTINE WARRIORS
Courageous Women Who Fought Fascism

Hannah Senesh

Hannah Senesh was born into a family that had been almost completely assimilated into Hungarian culture, but the Hungarian government's overt anti-Semitism in the late 1930s convinced her to become a Zionist at a young age. She moved to Palestine and became a member of a kibbutz there, but when she received news of Hitler's death camps in 1942, she joined an elite group of British-trained paratroopers. Their top-secret mission was to rescue trapped allied fliers and organize an escape network for those who would soon be deported to the camps. Along with thirty-one other Palestinian Jews, Senesh underwent rigorous training for over a year. She parachuted into Yugoslavia in March of 1944 and crossed into Hungary shortly before the German occupation there. She was eventually captured by the authorities, but although she was tortured, she would not divulge any information about her mission. Senesh was executed by firing squad in November of the same year. She was twenty-three.

Haviva Reik

Like Hannah Senesh, Reik emigrated to Palestine in the late 1930s. Reik was a native of Slovakia; the recent autonomy of the land of her birth had been supported by the Nazi government, which later occupied it. (Today, Slovakia is a part of the Czech and Slovak Federal Republic, more commonly known as Czechoslovakia.) A member of kibbutz Ma'anit, Reik and three other volunteers parachuted into their former homeland in 1944. Their aim was to conduct a wide variety of sabotage operations, support Jewish resistance to the occupation, and gather intelligence for the Allied forces. Reik was eventually captured in battle by German military authorities and executed. In present-day Israel, the kibbutz Lehavot Haviva and the Givat Havivah research center both bear her name in tribute to her courage.

Zivia Lubetkin

In 1943, Lubetkin was a member and a commander of a Jewish resistance movement in the Warsaw Ghetto. She fought courageously until the bitter end; as the Nazis approached, she fled via the Warsaw sewers with a handful of other survivors. Once on the "Aryan" side of the city, Lubetkin continued to risk her life by working with the Polish underground until the end of the war.

HANNAH SENESH

COMPROMISE DECLINED
Women Who Stood on Principle

Kasia

Kasia, a ninth-century poetess, was of noble blood, and was apparently in line for ascension to the Byzantine throne. During a "bride show" for the Emperor Theophilus, however, the monarch made a joke about all the world's evils issuing from women. Her indignant response was enough to insure her fall from the hierarchy.

Frances Anne Kemble

When this young Englishwoman was courted by a wealthy American in the 1830s, she was counseled by friends to avoid the marriage. Pierce Butler, they said, was not her equal intellectually—and she knew so little about him. She married him anyway, expecting a quiet life and the opportunity to pursue her passion in life, writing. The free-thinking Kemble discovered to her horror that she had married a slaveholding plantation owner—and one who viewed her impassioned pleas that he release his "property" with complete befuddlement. She kept a number of journals on contemporary American life and tried to have her observations published, but her husband, appalled at her liberal ideas, intervened. Kemble considered leaving Butler, but eventually returned and abandoned the project. (She was pregnant and had no money at the time.) She continued with her journals and letters, however, documenting with methodical thoroughness the inhuman treatment of her husband's slaves. Eventually the couple divorced, and Kemble was finally able to publish—over two decades after it had been completed—her antislavery tract, *Journal of a Residence on a Georgia Plantation*. It served as an effective piece of Union propaganda during the Civil War.

Jeannette Rankin

Rankin, a Montana Democrat, was elected to the U.S. House of Representatives in 1916, thereby becoming the first woman elected to the U.S. Congress. Her open opposition to United States involvement in World War I, however, led to her defeat in an attempt to win a seat in the U.S. Senate in 1918. Of her antiwar vote, she said later, "I felt . . . that the first woman [elected to the House of Representatives] should take the first stand, that the first time the first woman had a chance to say no to war, she should say it." Montanans returned Rankin to the House in 1940; on December 8, 1941, hers was the only dissenting vote to the U.S. declaration of war

JANET COLLINS

against Japan. She completed her remarkable record of dissent by leading the Jeannette Rankin Brigade on a Washington, D.C., protest march against the Vietnam War in 1968.

Janet Collins

As a young African-American dancer, Janet Collins made a choice that could have ended her career before it began. Collins was offered a position with prestigious Ballet Russe de Monte Carlo; the offer required Collins to wear white makeup to hide her African-American skin. She bluntly refused and walked away from the opportunity. Collins went on to a successful career both as a soloist and as a member of the Katherine Dunham ensemble. She eventually became the prima ballerina for the New York Metropolitan Opera.

CREDIT DENIED
Acclaim Given to Men
Instead of Women

Anna Ella Carroll

Her tombstone reads, "Maryland's Most Distinguished Lady. A great humanitarian and a close friend of Abraham Lincoln." This is true as far as it goes, but Carroll's service to the nation went considerably beyond her work as a pamphleteer for the president. She was the author of the Union's Tennessee campaign, but her postwar pleas for compensation and recognition for this fact fell on deaf ears. She received no medals or pension for her work. Carroll was one of the Union side's brilliant military strategists, but she was not one of its men. Accordingly, she was ignored. She died poor and anonymous in 1893.

Georgia "Tiny" Broadwick

In 1914, Broadwick was demonstrating air-jumping techniques to the U.S. Army in San Diego, California. After having problems with her automatic parachute on a previous jump, she pulled her release manually—thereby becoming the first person to make an intentional free-fall parachute jump from an airplane. No one noticed. Mr. Leslie Irvine did it five years later and received national acclaim.

Sophie Germain

This French mathematician's early work in the field of elasticity was influential and far-reaching, but, as the book *Women of Mathematics* points out, "when the Eiffel Tower was built, her name was not among those researchers in elasticity listed at its base as making possible its construction." It should have been; her research was one of the key contributions that made construction of the breakthrough structure possible.

Mary Leakey

Louis Leakey was celebrated the world over for discovering the skull of the 1.75 million year old "missing link" in July of 1959 in the Olduvai Gorge of present-day Tanzania. The find turned the scientific world upside down, as it demonstrated that early man had come from Africa, not Asia—and much earlier than had been supposed. It was not until years later that it was learned that the person who actually located the skull was not Mr. Leakey at all but his wife Mary. A quiet, supporting woman,

MARY LEAKEY

she was content to let her husband assume the mantle of glory. Widowed in 1972, Mrs. Leakey remained in Tanzania as Director of the Olduvai Gorge excavations, and eventually earned recognition in her own right as a leading authority on prehistoric cultures and technology.

Lena Jordan

In 1897, she became the first person to successfully complete the triple somersault on the flying trapeze. Unfortunately, modern record books listed trapezist Ernest Clarke as the holder of that title for years even though he completed his somersault a decade after Jordan. The record books were not alone in their error. Trapeze instructor Eddie Ward, oblivious to Jordan's accomplishment, wouldn't let his female students attempt the difficult move because he thought it was impossible for women. It was not until 1975 that the *Guiness Book of World Records* acknowledged Lena Jordan and even then it read: "Triple back somersault (female) 1897. Triple back somersault (male) 1909." It is only recently that she is listed alone.

DON'T TREAD ON ME
Women Best Not Trifled With

Queen Boudicca

Queen Boudicca of Britain was described by the historian Dio as "huge of frame, terrifying of aspect . . . (with) a great mass of red hair." When the Romans demanded, around 59 A.D., the repayment of funds given as a grant to her late husband King Prasutagus, she refused. As a result, she was flogged by Roman kidnapers, and her daughters were publicly raped. Apparently believing they had taught the monarch a lesson, the Romans let her live—a mistake, as she was bent on revenge. Boudicca called the many small kingdoms on the island to unity, mustered a massive army, and led a methodical wave of butchery southward to London. She countenanced unspeakable atrocities against the Romans and their allies, mutilating and skewering her opponents by the hundreds. Boudicca nearly carried the day, but her troops were disorganized, and she fell to Roman forces despite an overwhelming numerical advantage. She and her daughters committed suicide before they could be taken by the enemy.

Hannah Duston

The Abnakis tribe was often incited by the French to attack English settlements in the Massachusetts Bay Colony, but when they raided Haverhill on March 15, 1697, and murdered Hannah Duston's week-old baby, they made what proved to be a grave mistake. Duston and nurse Mary Neff, taken hostage, were marched to a small New Hampshire island and told to prepare themselves to be stripped naked and whipped. On the island, however, they encountered another hostage, an English boy named Samuel Lennardson. Under the cover of night, Lennardson and Duston stole some hatchets and killed all ten of their captors. Duston accounted for nine of the Abnakis fatalities. The three former captives secured a boat and made their escape, but Hannah then decided to turn back on her own to collect the scalps of the ten tribesmen. Her proof of the encounter won her and her two companions a hefty cash reward from the General Court in Boston.

ANNE BONNY

Anne Bonny

A legendary pirate, Bonny was definitely not to be trifled with. When her father disinherited her in 1715, she burned down his plantation and fled to the present-day Bahamas. As she attempted to disembark, a one-eared sailor attempted to block her way, demanding that she have a drink with him. She drew her pistol and blasted off his other ear. The crew stared at the scene, amazed. "By God," Bonny howled, "is that a head? I thought I was shooting the handle off a mug." (Bonny was the lover of Mary Read; see *Gender Benders*, page 44–45.)

DRAWING THE LINE
Women in the World of Cartooning

Rose O'Neill

They started out as cute little drawings of cherubs, but cartoonist Rose O'Neill wondered if they might be something more. In 1913, the Kewpie Doll craze made her a millionaire. The dolls' legions of fans worldwide also bought them in the form of cards, soap, and even salt-and-pepper shakers. The adorable Kewpie kids, perhaps the first great character merchandising phenomenon, were originally based on a sketch of O'Neill's baby brother.

Marge

Her pen name was succinct and to the point, and so was her style. Marge Henderson Buell developed the long-running strip *Little Lulu* in the mid-1930s and gave the world a whirlwind of precocious cartoon trouble not to be equaled until Hank Ketchum's *Dennis the Menace* took off in the 1950s. *Little Lulu* was a huge hit that continued in various forms for three decades; in fact, Lulu was so popular that Marge was unable to keep up with the public's appetite for her feisty little girl. In various incarnations and formats over the years—comic books, advertisements, and later versions of the newspaper strip—Lulu's adventures were managed by a string of male cartoonists duplicating the style of the initial creator of the strip, who was able to retire with the series still quite popular.

Edwina Dumm

Edwina Dumm, who began working for the Columbus (Ohio) *Monitor* in 1915, is believed to be the first female editorial cartoonist in history. Her work, done in the heavily metaphoric style of the day, is still quite impressive both for the issues it tackled and the technical merit it displayed. Dumm, who was only 22 when she began working professionally, covered overseas conflicts, women's suffrage issues, and domestic political squabbles large and small. Her work received what was doubtless meant to be high praise when she was profiled in a professional cartoonists' journal as follows: "No subject is too big for her to wrestle with, and in the pages of the *Monitor* she interprets world events in real masculine cartoons."

EDWINA DUMM

Dale Messick

She began her attempt to break into syndicated cartooning by distributing her cartoons under her given name: Dalia Messick. Editors were less than receptive, so she changed her first name to the more androgynous "Dale." It worked. She began getting work and eventually launched her strip *Brenda Starr* on June 29th, 1940. Now in the capable hands of artist Ramona Fradon and writer Mary Schmich, the legendary strip has entered its fifty-second year.

"E" FOR ESPIONAGE
Fighting the Secret Battles of World War II

Christine Granville (Countess Skarbek)
This former Miss Poland, one of the most artful manipulators in World War II espionage, is credited with convincing a German garrison of Polish troops to surrender on the Italian border. Granville also saved the lives of two fellow agents by bluffing their Gestapo captors into releasing the captives only hours before they were scheduled to be executed. She was known for her dedication to the safety of those who risked their lives to work with her; not one of her contacts was caught by the Germans.

Anne Brusselsmans
Brusselsmans, an Englishwoman living in Belgium, put her own life in jeopardy to save the lives of American and British airmen. Throughout the war, this homemaker and mother of two used her apartment in Brussels as a part of an escape line, supervising the passage of more than 150 Allied airmen out of Nazi-controlled territory. Her apartment was searched by the Gestapo several times, but the Germans never managed to find the evidence against her they were looking for.

Germaine Devalet
This courageous Belgian woman offered shelter to anyone fleeing the Gestapo; she also worked in a clandestine news network, intercepting German radio messages and helping to disseminate anti-Axis bulletins. She was arrested in 1943 and died while incarcerated at the infamous Ravensbruck Concentration Camp.

Katherina Zalenska

Zalenska, who grew up as a Polish Jew during the Second World War, knew hardship first-hand. When she was twenty, Katherina and her sister were separated from their parents; her father was murdered at Katyn Wood and her mother was deported to the Gobi Desert. The sisters began to work as couriers for the Polish resistance, taking documents through German-occupied territory into Hungary. On one mission, Katherina and her sister were stopped and held by the Nazis, but they fooled the Gestapo into thinking they were harmless schoolgirls. Katherina continued to work as a courier while training to be a nurse. During the Warsaw

CHRISTINE GRANVILLE

seige in 1944, she helped survivors of the Nazi onslaught escape and was twice decorated for valor. After the war, she continued to study nursing, but because of a severe shortage of physicians she was trained to do some emergency work, including surgery. In 1956, when Poles were finally allowed exit visas, Katherina learned that her mother was alive and in London and relocated to England. She obtained a position at St. James Hospital. In 1959, she decided to leave Europe for good, settling in Nigeria.

ELEANOR'S CABINET
Important Women of the Roosevelt Administration

Note: In 1933, Franklin D. Roosevelt took office as President of the United States. His administration was a remarkable one from the standpoint of women's rights, and particularly for its elevation to national status of a select group of women reformers and activists. Accustomed to being "outside the loop," a number of brilliant women with extensive experience in social welfare issues suddenly found themselves with access to the country's highest levels of political power. There were two reasons for this. First, their skills, abilities, and contacts provided a natural match with the objectives of the fledgling New Deal. Second, FDR's wife and political confidant Eleanor Roosevelt, who was about to turn the position of First Lady from benign symbol to active and intellectually vigorous power center, was, as historian Sara Evans points out, "one of them."

Molly Dewson
Franklin Roosevelt appointed Dewson, an old friend and ally of the First Lady, to head the Women's Division of the Democratic National Committee. She served as a rich source of leads for qualified women Eleanor could recommend to FDR for party and administration positions, and was the National Democratic Party's first great organizer of women voters.

Frances Perkins

Perkins had conducted an influential survey on New York's notorious Hell's Kitchen district while completing work on her master's degree from Columbia. In 1918, she received an appointment to New York State's Industrial Commission; this marked the beginning of a successful career in government. She was named to head the board in 1926 by New York governor Al Smith, and continued to hold the post under the state's next governor, Franklin Roosevelt. Perkins was a tireless advocate for the health and safety of American workers, and female workers in particular. (She had been an eyewitness to the horrific Triangle Shirtwaist Fire of 1911 that killed 146

MARY MCLEOD BETHUNE

workers, mostly women.) Her nomination as Secretary of Labor in 1933 made Perkins the first woman ever named to a cabinet post.

Mary McLeod Bethune

Bethune, the foremost black educator of her day, served as Negro Affairs Director for the National Youth Administration from 1936 to 1944. That was her official title; unofficially, she also served as leader of the "Black Cabinet," a group of African-American officials in key federal positions who advised the White House informally on a wide variety of issues. Her work proceeded along much the same lines as that of Dewson, Perkins, and Eleanor Roosevelt, but was, in keeping with the attitudes of the time, limited to the concerns of those of her own race.

ELECTORAL FIRSTS
Pioneering Female Officeholders

Lydia Hasbrouck

A school board election may not seem like a history-making event, but it was in March of 1880. That's when reformer Lydia Hasbrouck, who had vowed to "stand or fall in the battle for women's physical, political, and educational freedom and equality," won election to the Middletown (New York) School Board. She was the first American woman to hold elected office.

Susanna Medora Salter

On the fourth of April, 1887, Susanna Salter went to cast her vote in the local Argonia, Kansas, elections, and was stunned by what she read at the polls. Salter found her own name on the ballot as a candidate for mayor, although she had never expressed any intention to run for the office. Unbeknownst to her, a local women's temperance organization had nominated her and somehow overlooked telling the candidate of her status. Salter—who had not campaigned—carried the town handily and was thus elected the first woman mayor in the United States. She served for one year.

Nellie Ross

Ross, of Wyoming, was the first female governor in United States history. She was the wife of the state's Democratic governor William Ross; when he died unexpectedly in 1924, party leaders asked Nellie to head the state ticket. She won handily and served a model first term, reducing state debt by over $1 million and improving performance in public education. She lost her bid for re-election in 1926, but was later named the first female director of the United States Mint by President Franklin D. Roosevelt.

Bertha Landes

In 1924, Landes was a reform-minded Seattle city council president who proved her mettle by cracking down on gambling houses and ridding the town payroll of corrupt officials. When she ran for the mayor's office in 1926, she stunned the nation by winning—and becoming the nation's first female big-city mayor. She served one efficient term and is still regarded as one of the finest public servants ever to have held Seattle's top job.

NELLIE ROSS

AN EYE TO THE HEAVENS
Early Female Religious Leaders

Anne Hutchinson

A follower of clergyman John Cotton, this brilliant woman mounted an unprecedented challenge against the Puritan hierarchy of the Massachusetts colony in the 1630s. She drew large numbers of men and women to her home to hear her discourse on the "doctrine of grace." Her teachings charged Puritan religious leaders with laying too much emphasis on the external trappings of salvation and underemphasizing the importance of an inner relationship with God—a relationship beyond the concept of salvation "earned" by means of good works. This challenge of clerical authority—and the immense political implications it carried in the fledgling colony—quickly earned Hutchinson a wave of legal assaults meant to silence her. But the trials she underwent were not the simple matters her accusers might have expected. She engaged no less a figure than the colonial governor, John Winthrop, in a series of remarkable exchanges in which she matched her accusers biblical citation for biblical citation. Her astonished accusers shifted gears and charged her with what she was manifestly engaged in: acting outside the sphere of endeavor allowed to women by Puritan society. "You have stepped out of your place," charged interrogator Hugh Peter. "You have rather been a husband than a wife, and a preacher than a hearer, and a magistrate than a subject." When Hutchinson claimed to have received a direct revelation from God, she was immediately excommunicated. She lived in a number of other colonies after her banishment, and was eventually killed in an Indian raid. Hers was the first real challenge to religious intolerance in American history.

Mother Ann Lee

The founding mother of the Shaker sect, Lee was believed by thousands to be the female incarnation of Jesus Christ. The Shaker religion, which advocated complete celibacy among members, excellence in all endeavors, and intense devotion to rituals of community, was begun as an offshoot of the Quakers by this intensely religious and independent-minded woman. She spent two years in prison in England for challenging religious authorities there, then emigrated to the United States in 1774 believing firmly in her own divinity. Her movement grew by adopting orphans and eventually boasted eighteen prosperous communities in eight states. The number

ANNE HUTCHINSON

of Shakers eventually dwindled to almost nothing by the end of the nineteenth century, but in their heyday the group was one of the most successful of the era's many utopian experiments. The Shakers were notable for their insistence on the dual nature of the Deity: male and female.

Barbara R. Heck

Heck, having been converted to Methodism by John Wesley in 1753, brought her religious zeal to the colonies. Her first meeting consisted of four people in her cousin's home; from this humble beginning came the first Methodist church in the New World. Heck later founded the first Canadian Methodist church. A Tory supporter, she left the colonies during the American Revolution.

FOUNDING MOTHERS
Women Who Created New Nations

Himiko, Queen of Wa
This fourth-century monarch, who united dozens of warring clans into a single national unit, is recognized as the first person on record to rule what we now know as Japan. She sent a group of envoys to Chinese rulers and was succeeded by her thirteen-year-old relative Toyo as queen.

Trung Trai and Trung Nhi
When Vietnam was conquered by the Chinese in 111 B.C., the existing matrifocal culture was dismantled. ("Matrifocal" means that family units are centered around mothers, with fathers largely absent from the social order.) In 40 A.D., these two sisters raised an army of 80,000 troops, commanded by female generals and won back Vietnamese autonomy—briefly. After sharing political power for three years, Trung Trai and Trung Nhi were overthrown. They committed suicide rather than submit to their Chinese conquerors, but are remembered as among the first Vietnamese to struggle victoriously against Chinese invasion.

Mana Ocllo
Together with her three sisters and four brothers, Mana Ocllo was one of the founders of the Incan empire in present-day Peru. She and her husband/brother Manco Copac were the progenitors of the Inca ruling line.

Queen Eire

Eire, leader of the Tuatha de Danaan (which translates as People of the Goddess Dana), was a warrior-queen who mustered a powerful military force against the invading Milesians before 400 B.C. It is in her honor that her kingdom, which we know as Ireland, is named.

Nadezhda Krupskaya, Inessa Armand, and Clara Zetkin

The wife of Bolshevik leader Vladimir I. Lenin, Krupskaya published *The Woman Worker* in the years leading up to the October Revolution of 1917.

NADEZHDA KRUPSKAYA

Together with Armand and Zetkin, she successfully lobbied for observance of International Women's Day, which was first celebrated in Russia. Four years after the holiday's first observance, on International Women's Day, 1917, it was the demonstrations of women textile workers—which grew into bread riots—that sparked the Russian Revolution.

FROM THE GROUND UP
Women in Design and Construction

Hannah Clapp

How did Hannah Clapp win the contract to build the massive, elaborate iron fence that surrounds Nevada's capitol all the way back in 1875? Well, she started out by knowing what she was up against: She submitted her bid under the craftily ambiguous name H.K. Clapp. That got her in the door. Then it was just a matter of coming up with the best design, meeting all the technical requirements, and significantly underbidding her many male competitors. She did all three, and, having won the job, personally supervised the five-year project.

Lady Deborah Moody

Moody, an eloquent and educated eighteenth-century woman who was probably the first modern city planner, had the foresight to recognize the importance of organizing urban areas before they began to grow haphazardly. She gained experience in designing cities by laying out villages in her native England, but fled as a result of religious persecution and eventually settled in what is now New York State. She acquired the regions today known as Coney Island, Sheepshead, Bensonhurst and Midwood, and designed the towns from the ground up before they were heavily developed. Her neatly organized grid systems are still evident in the towns' street designs.

Julia Morgan

Julia Morgan had designed over 1,000 buildings when William Randolph Hearst chose her to be the architect for his massive California castle, San Simeon, 1919. Hearst requested a home that was both "elegant and comfortable" by his standards; price was not a consideration. The publishing magnate provided Morgan with a list of what the house needed: "100 rooms, an 83-foot assembly hall, 31 bathrooms, two libraries, and a garage for 25 limousines." It was Morgan who turned this laundry-list into a technically feasible project—and ultimately into one of the most famous design and construction projects of the twentieth century.

EMILY ROEBLING

Emily Roebling

She was the wife of Brooklyn Bridge chief engineer Washington Roebling, and was his eyes and ears during the final stages of construction. With her husband confined to a bed in the project's last years, Roebling served as *de facto* overseer, tirelessly conducting independent interviews with the major contractors, assessing progress on-site, and faithfully reporting all the details of the massive project's final days to her husband. Mr. Roebling considered his wife "invaluable" during the last years of the project and praised her remarkable talent as a peacemaker on the hectic, often tumultuous job. At his request, Emily Roebling was the first person to cross the span when it finally opened in 1883. At the time of that historic crossing, the Brooklyn Bridge was the longest suspension bridge in human history.

FRONT-PAGE NEWS
Trailblazing Journalists

Ann Franklin
Franklin, sister-in-law of Benjamin Franklin, became editor of the Newport, Rhode Island, *Mercury* when her husband died in 1762. She was also the colony's main printer for at least eleven years. Her obituary reported that she had, "by her economy and industry . . . supported herself and family, and brought up her children in a genteel manner . . . . She was a woman of great integrity and uprightness in her station and conversation, and was well beloved in the town."

Ida B. Wells-Barnett
This remarkable turn-of-the-century black journalist carried out a trailblazing study of lynchings in the South that indicated that most of the murders did not represent white retribution for sexual assaults by black men on white women, as was commonly believed. Instead, Wells-Barnett reported, the typical lynching victim had somehow posed an *economic* threat to white male social structures, whether through individual enterprise or, not infrequently, blind luck. Her findings, initially ignored, were confirmed decades later by independent researchers.

Adela Rogers St. Johns
Being an investigative reporter in the twenties and thirties for Hearst Publications was a dangerous job, especially when covering your beat meant exposing the shenanigans of powerful people. That didn't seem to bother Adela Rogers St. Johns. On more than one occasion she took on top-level officials in the Los Angeles city government; in the

1920s she exposed widespread corruption among their top ranks. To bring to light Los Angeles' neglect of its poor, St. Johns borrowed a costume from the M-G-M's studios and disguised herself as an impoverished women in search of employment. St. Johns, whose first story was printed when she was nine years old in 1903, covered some of the biggest stories of the twentieth century: the Lindbergh kidnaping trial, Edward VIII's abdication and marriage to Wallace Simpson, and even the Patty Hearst ordeal in 1976.

IDA B. WELLS-BARNETT

Dorothy Thompson

Thompson was the most prominent woman journalist of the 1930s; she was an acknowledged expert in foreign affairs who often covered her European beat despite official disapproval of her stories. Adolf Hitler ordered her out of Germany in 1934, but even this did not stop her from reporting on the alarming developments in Nazi Germany. *Time* magazine considered Thompson to be the second-most-influential woman in the country (behind Eleanor Roosevelt) in 1939.

Doris Fleeson

The scourge of four Administrations, Fleeson was acknowledged as one of the very toughest journalists in Washington in the forties, fifties, and early sixties. She was the first female political columnist, and she won the bewildered admiration of her male counterparts (many of whom she treated with open contempt) for her objectivity, straight-ahead prose style, and incomparably unforgiving analyses of public figures. President John F. Kennedy once went on record as preferring to be lambasted by powerhouse *New York Times* columnist Arthur Krock than to fall into disfavor with Doris Fleeson.

GENDER BENDERS
Women Who Won Autonomy
by Taking Male Identities

Doña Catalina de Erauso

This Spanish nobleman's daughter, born in 1592, was reportedly given to a nearby convent as an infant—her family already had two daughters and saw no need for more. She never took to religious life, and at age fifteen she cut her hair, disguised herself as a boy, and ran away. This marked the beginning of a remarkable career as an accomplished cross-dressing swords"man," bandit, and mercenary in Spain and Latin America. She won honors for her battlefield exploits from the King of Spain and the Pope. She left a trail of duels, battles, and brushes with the law throughout Europe and the New World before she died in 1650.

Mary Read

Read took the identity of "Mark Read" in the early 1700s to secure a position as a merchant seaman. When her ship was taken by a band of pirates, she continued the charade and took up life as a "male" pirate herself. Read fell in with the notorious woman pirate Anne Bonny (see *Don't Tread on Me*, page 27) and Bonny's male lover, Calico Jack. Bonny seems to have taken an instant liking to Read, and probably knew of her true identity before they went to sea. In any event, a jealous and suspicious Calico Jack believed his rival for Bonny's attentions to be a male; he burst in upon the two and found the indisputably female Read sprawled naked on Bonny's bed. That ended the mystery—and apparently marked the beginning of an open relationship between the two women that no one in their circle dared challenge. Bonny and Read conducted a spirited career of thievery and plunder on the high seas that ended, not surprisingly, in their capture and conviction in 1720.

Sara Edmonds

Edmonds, who fought in the first Battle of Bull Run and performed key espionage work for the North, was one of approximately 400 women who disguised themselves as male Union soldiers to assume combat duty in the Civil War. (Curiously, there is no record of any Confederate women having taken such steps.) Among the reasons forwarded by scholars for the cross-dressing phenomenon are the desire to be near beloved husbands, and intense Union patriotism.

DONA CATALINA DE ERAUSO

"Dr. James Barry"

It is unlikely we will ever know this remarkable woman's given name, but what we do know about her is this: She enrolled as a male at Edinburgh University in 1810 to study medicine and maintained a virtually perfect masquerade as a male doctor until her death fifty-five years later. A charwoman preparing the body for the funeral was the first person on record as discovering the doctor's true gender. Barry's career in the British colonies culminated in "his" appointment as Inspector General of the British Army medical department in Canada.

THE GODMOTHERS
Women in Organized Crime

Catherine Monvoisin

As an apothecary and a practitioner of black magic, Monvoisin established a "sinister web of witchery" that won many followers. Among the practices of her group was dispensing "love-potions and poisons" to various seventeenth-century French noblewomen in the court of Louis XIV. The poisons were meant to help rid the user of unwanted husbands, lovers, or adversaries. Upon the king's request, an investigation into the Monvoisin group was conducted; roughly 400 people were found to be involved in the deadly network. Over thirty of the Monvoisonites were sentenced to death; a similar number were imprisoned indefinitely. Catherine, the leader of the operation, was burned at the stake in 1680.

Molly Frith

She wouldn't go to school. She wouldn't go to work as a servant. Molly Frith was, to put it bluntly, a juvenile delinquent, even though the term did not exist in the London of the 1590s. Accordingly, she set out on a life of crime and became one of Britain's most infamous—and powerful—outlaws. English authorities succeeded in putting her in prison for wounding a prestigious military figure during a robbery at Hounslow Heath, but she slipped out again by making a huge direct payment to the victim from her ample coffers. She continued to make a good living at violent crime, commanding a large gang of thieves. Eventually she opened a pawnshop where robbery victims could, by a remarkable coincidence, often find stolen goods to buy back. Frith lived to the age of 75, uncommon for the era. She was celebrated in song and story as "Moll Cutpurse."

Mary Butterworth

While most New England colonial women were making meals in their kitchens, Mary Butterworth was making money. Literally. In 1716, she began her first attempts at producing exact duplicates of bills of credit, undertaking the operation with the help of family members as well as prominent local figures such as the Town Clerk of her home town of Rehoboth, Massachusetts. Butterworth was able to mass-produce and successfully distribute eight different varieties of bills. In 1723, suspicious authorities arrested the members of the group. Due to a lack of physical evidence and the unbroken code of silence maintained by the principals, however, they were all released.

MOLLY FRITH

Lucretia "Patty" Cannon

Cannon was the scourge of 1820s Reliance, Delaware, where she ran a tavern that was the nerve center of a crime operation as brutal as it was ambitious. Cannon herself murdered at least eleven people, one of whom was her own unfortunate husband. Most despicable of her gang's activities was probably its systematic kidnaping of free blacks who were later sold into slavery. Cannon's tavern was the place to go if you were a slave trader in search of new human "merchandise." She was arrested and convicted in 1829, but she committed suicide before the death sentence that had been handed down against her could be carried out.

THE GOOD EARTH
Agricultural Pioneers

Julia Tuttle

In a few short years Tuttle turned 640 acres of unappealing, barren Florida wilderness into a sea of productive citrus, floral, and vegetable croplands. A force to be reckoned with in 1890s Florida, she was one of the few farmers whose orange blossoms survived the killing freeze of 1894-1895. Tuttle was also the mother of present-day Miami: she put her considerable resources and persuasive ability to the task of persuading developer Henry Flagler to run his railroad line from Palm Beach to southern Florida, and even deeded him half of her holdings as an incentive. Tuttle was the first person to see the vast agricultural potential of the region; a major thoroughfare in the area is named in her honor.

Eliza Tibbetts

Whether she acted alone or with her husband is still a matter of some debate, but however you look at it the American fruit industry owes a lot to Eliza Tibbetts. In 1873—so the most popular version of the story goes—Mrs. Tibbetts acquired two newly budded Bahia navel trees and planted them in Riverside, California. These served as the parent trees of the popular navel orange family that has yielded literally billions of seedless fruit. One of the trees is still alive; it is said to represent the single-most-valuable fruit introduction in world agricultural history.

Freda Ehmann

It is no exaggeration to say that Ehmann more or less invented the California olive industry. She turned her modest twenty-acre spread into the first modern olive processing plant. Along the way she founded the Ehmann Olive Products Company. She died in 1932, and is still known fondly as the Mother of the California Ripe Olive.

FREDA EHMANN

HISTORY OR HIS STORY?
Some Underexamined Achievements

Pope Joan

Was there a female pope named Joan in the ninth century? A fifteenth-century historical chronicle unambiguously listed her as the successor to Leo IV, who died in 855. The *Nuremberg Chronicle* of 1493, which has been frequently suppressed or altered in the centuries following its official release, features a painting of Joan and her baby, whose birth is listed as the event that revealed Joan's female identity and led to her death by stoning in 858. (She had, the *Chronicle* relates, assumed office under the name "John VIII.") Other references to Joan date back to the eleventh century, but contemporary references to Joan are lacking. The name of this "mystery pope" was officially changed to Zachary in 1600, and Joan's story was declared to be mythical by Pope Clement VIII in 1601.

Mileva Maric

Albert Einstein's first wife, Mileva, was a talented physicist and mathematician in her own right. Some researchers feel she may have made major contributions to her husband's development of the theory of relativity. Maryland physicist and researcher Evan Harris Walker argues that Mileva may even have served as a full collaborator on three historic 1905 papers, including the one that won Mr. Einstein the 1921 Nobel Prize in Physics. The evidence: approximately a dozen passages in Einstein's pre-1905 letters to his wife referring to the papers as "our work" and (to some) strongly suggestive of an intimate working relationship between the two. One 1901 letter reads, "How happy and proud I will be when the two of us together have brought our work on the relative motion to a victorious conclusion!" Mr. Einstein gave Mileva all the proceeds from his 1921 Nobel Prize. Some argue that this was part of the couple's divorce settlement, but Mileva was already provided for at the time of Einstein's release of the (as yet theoretical) prize money. The notion that Einstein may have worked closely with his wife on this monumental theory has not been a popular one in the scientific community. Unfortunately, the original manuscripts of the papers—which could settle the question—have been lost.

DR. MARY EDWARDS WALKER

Dr. Mary Edwards Walker

Honored by President Andrew Johnson with the Medal of Honor for her outstanding medical work on the battlefields of the Civil War, Walker was stripped of the honor in 1917 on the grounds that existing records did not show "the specific act or acts for which the decoration was originally awarded." This was tenuous at best, as Walker had achieved national recognition for her work with the 52nd Ohio Infantry Division. (Some feel her unapologetic and lifelong transvestism may have been a factor that shocked the later generation of lawmakers.) In what Walker's supporters through the years viewed as a travesty of her memory, the medal was not reinstated until 1977, 60 years after the death of the woman who earned it.

HORSING AROUND
Famous Early Female Rodeo Stars

Bertha Kaepernick

In the 1890s, Kaepernick became the first female entrant in a rodeo. The Wyoming woman braved muddy conditions so bad that her male counterparts at first demanded that the bucking bronco competition be postponed. Bertha had other ideas. A published report written by one of the spectators at the Cheyenne Frontier Days described Kaepernick's remarkable ride: "(The horse was) one of the worst buckers I have ever seen—and she stayed on him all the time. Part of the time he was up in the air on his hind feet; once he fell backward, and the girl deftly slid to one side only to mount him again as he got up. She rode him in the mud to a finish, and the crowd went wild . . . . The real active idea of Woman Suffrage was thus demonstrated in Wyoming . . . the idea that has gone around the world. Hurrah for the Wyoming gals! They lead in everything!"

Tillie Baldwin

In addition to introducing the Roman Stand, a death-defying maneuver that was later adopted by many other rodeo professionals, Baldwin was the first woman to bulldog steers in competition. She was also noted for helping to introduce rodeo attire that made a more dramatic statement than the typical cowboy attire of blue jeans and buckskins. Tillie opted for fringed leather outfits with lots of brightly colored ornaments. Like the rodeo stars who followed, she didn't mean to be missed in a crowd.

Lucille Mulhall

Not many rodeo stars can claim to have roped a coyote for a President of the United States, but Mulhall was not just any rodeo star. Theodore Roosevelt, who was visiting his father's ranch, once sat in at a rodeo in which Mulhall was competing and blithely asked whether she could lasso a coyote while riding her horse. She could—and did.

Tad Lucas

Lucas, the youngest of twenty-four children fathered by the first white settler in Cody, Nebraska, is generally acknowledged as one of the greatest trick riders—male or female—in history. She won

TAD LUCAS

the prestigious competitions at the Madison Square Garden Rodeo eight times in the late twenties and early thirties, and was the recipient of hundreds of other trophies from United States and international competitions. When she broke her arm in a serious riding accident in 1933, her doctor told her the arm would have to be amputated and that she would never ride again. She proved him wrong: three months later, she was performing wearing a heavy cast and guiding her horse with her good arm.

INAPPROPRIATE ATTIRE
Women Who Wore What They Pleased

Lady Hester Stanhope

Lady Hester was raised in an isolated, upper-class English environment. She was an eager supporter and dispenser of patronage for her uncle, Prime Minister William Pitt the Younger, but when he died in 1806, she decided to travel. In 1810, she left England—permanently, as it turned out—and made her way through the Mediterranean. When she reached Turkey, she assumed the garb of a Turkish man: roomy pants, silk turban, a colorful shirt. British officials got wind of this and, hearing she was bound for Damascus, panicked. Lady Hester was warned that for her to appear in a city like Damascus, where Moslem law required that every woman appear discreetly veiled, would incite riots. She went anyway, charmed the crowds (an ability she would continue to use to her advantage for decades), and began a series of desert exploits that culminated in a remarkable, unchallenged personal empire of sorts based in Dar Djoun. Author Malcolm Forbes, writing a century later, would call Stanhope "the female Lawrence of Arabia."

Annie Smith Peck

Peck, the first woman to reach the peak of the Matterhorn and the first mountaineer of either sex to reach the top of 21,812-foot Mount Huascaran in Peru, received almost as much press for her clothing as her derring-do. The press viewed her decision to wear a pair of knickerbockers during an 1895 climb (rather than a set of detachable skirts that fit over her pants) as a major news event. Previous female climbers had always worn floor-length skirts; one woman was even forced to scale the same peak twice in one day to retrieve the skirt she had left on the summit, since she refused to be seen entering an inn wearing only her climbing pants. Peck, who apparently realized the ridiculousness of attempting to scale a mountainside while restricting the freedom of movement of one's legs, decided she would have none of it. She received waves of derisive press attention, but her achievements eventually spoke louder than the sexist headlines. Peck continued to make major climbs well into her sixties.

ANNIE SMITH PECK

Eleanora Sears

Sears, an accomplished sportswoman who was a four-time National Women's Doubles tennis champion between 1911 and 1917, made headlines when she dared to roll up her sleeves during a match. That was nothing, however, compared to her 1912 jaunt across a field being used for a men's polo team practice. Sears wore jodhpurs and— *scandaleuse!*—rode astride her horse rather than sidesaddle. A shocked group of local mothers drew up a resolution requesting that she "restrict herself to the normal feminine attire." She ignored it.

IN THE SERVICE OF THE DISENFRANCHISED
Women Who Stood Up for Society's Forgotten Members

Lydia F. Child She was an established and comparatively successful writer of fiction whose life was changed forever when she met abolitionist leader William Lloyd Garrison in 1831. "(He) got hold of the strings of my conscience," she later wrote of the encounter, "and pulled me into reforms." She and her husband David became prominent in the abolitionist movement; Lydia began writing antislavery books, notably *An Appeal in Favor of That Class of Americans Called Africans*. This book was well reasoned and highly influential in persuading some leading social figures to join the cause, but it was a commercial disappointment—and it didn't do much for Lydia's status as a commercially viable novelist. The Childs were considered radicals and social outcasts, and Lydia's income plummeted, but the couple did not abandon their convictions. Although Lydia's career was uneven at best and the couple continually faced severe financial problems, she continued her work for the abolitionist cause in the decades preceding the Civil War. In one memorable response to a proslavery tract that lauded slaveholders' sensitivity to the "the pangs of maternity" of black mothers, Lydia noted that, in the North, " 'the pangs of maternity' . . . meet with the requisite assistance; and here [in New England], after we have helped the mothers, *we do not sell the babies.*"

Kate Waller Barrett Raised in an atmosphere of privilege, Barrett was one of the first vocal advocates for the plight of lower-income women faced with the burden of raising a child without a husband. At its base, her crusade was designed to help prostitutes find another way of life; those from whom she sought support in her efforts were usually shocked at her plans, suggesting she focus instead on helping unwed women of good reputation under the age of eighteen. But such a course did not resolve the problems Barrett had by now seen first-hand many times in Richmond and in Atlanta, where her supportive husband Robert, a prominent minister, was assigned. She won sympathy but no open support from her husband's ministerial colleagues; after months of wrangling, she

KATE WALLER BARRETT

finally managed to convince Atlanta's City Council to deed her a tract of land. That left her with the fundraising to manage; she appealed successfully to a wealthy New Yorker named Charles Crittendon for funding, and in 1893 opened the Florence Crittendon Home, named after Crittendon's late daughter. The mission was a success, and more than that: its central idea, that of keeping mother and child together, was a new and hugely influential concept in the development of later social welfare work in the new field Kate Barrett had opened.

Georgia Lusk Lusk was a legend in New Mexico politics; her career in public life spanned the mid-twenties to the late fifties. She was elected to Congress in 1946, but it was as state superintendent of public instruction—a post she held in various one-and two-term increments over the decades due to New Mexico's term limitation laws—that she made her mark. She was the person most responsible for the introduction of free textbooks to all New Mexico schools, and was a powerful force in convincing the state legislature to upgrade the state's substandard school facilities.

IN TIME OF CRISIS
Women Who Saved the Day

Artemisia of Halicarnassus
This fifth-century Greek woman, believed to be the first woman ever to captain a ship, had to take command of the five-craft fleet of her husband when he died in battle. Artemisia served as an important ally to Xerxes in the ocean battle of Marathon, and wreaked such havoc on the Athenians that they offered a sizable ransom to anyone who could take her prisoner. No one did.

Sybil Ludington
Most grade-school students are taught about the exploits of Paul Revere, who made his famous ride the night before the Battle of Lexington in 1775 to alert Massachusetts colonists of the approach of the British. Schoolchildren should probably hear a word or two about Sybil Ludington, as well. On the night of April 26, 1777, the sixteen-year-old patriot rode from town to town to tell New York and Connecticut colonists that the Redcoats had begun a raid on Danbury. She produced enough volunteers to help repel the British the next day. Sybil's ride covered double the distance of Revere's. Her home town in New York was renamed in her honor by grateful residents.

Grace Darling
Her father was lighthouse keeper at England's remote Farne Islands; in 1838, when a steamboat called *Forfarshire* went down nearby, Grace and her father rowed out in tumultuous conditions to retrieve five shivering survivors hanging for dear life to

a large rock. The father-and-daughter rescue squad were rewarded with medals and £1700 in cash by a grateful nation. Tragically, Grace died a few years later of consumption, at home on her island.

Sarah Rooke

In the late summer of 1908, torrential rains caused New Mexico's Cimmarron River to overflow its banks. Rooke was working as a telephone operator as the river swelled; she spent the terrifying afternoon and evening of August 27 calling as many of the imperiled residents of the small town of Folsom as she could, finally managing to alert and save all but eighteen of the town's residents. Sarah herself

SYBIL LUDINGTON

was among the fatalities of the great flood because she refused to leave her switchboard while fellow townspeople were unaccounted for. They found her body in the spring of the following year, eight miles downstream.

LET FREEDOM RING
Helping to Win the American Revolution

Mary Katherine Goddard
Her husband had made a mess of the family printing business, so it was Mary who ran the Baltimore shop that printed the newspaper *The Maryland Journal*—and, in 1776, a document entitled the Declaration of Independence. (Goddard, postmaster of Baltimore, was also the first woman to hold a federal job.)

Margaret Corbin
Corbin's husband John was killed in November of 1776 while he was manning a gunnery position near Fort Washington, New York, that came under Hessian attack. Margaret, who had traveled with her husband, bravely assumed his position in the battle but sustained serious injury in the process. When the Americans surrendered, she was not held as a prisoner. Gravely wounded, she traveled to Philadelphia, where her case came to the attention of the Continental Congress. She was granted a lifetime soldier's half-pay pension and was listed on military rolls until April 1783, a first for an American woman.

Deborah Sampson
Sampson was the first woman to enlist in the American armed forces. Under the name Robert Shurtlieff, she disguised herself as a man to serve in the 4th Massachusetts Regiment in 1782. She was twice wounded in battle, first by a saber in a skirmish near Tarrytown, New York, and then by a musket shot near East Chester. The second wound was serious, but she attended to it herself rather than risk reveal-

ing her true identity. She was awarded a full pension from Congress in September of 1818. Today a monument to her stands in her home town of Sharon, Massachusetts.

Lydia Barrington Darragh

The British who occupied Lydia Darragh's home in Philadelphia on the night of December 2, 1777, did not anticipate that the lady of the house would listen at the keyhole, memorize the details of their forthcoming plan of attack against Washington's army, and then (under the pretext of buying flour at an out-of-town mill) sped to the American general's position at Whitemarsh to alert him. This she did,

DEBORAH SAMPSON

and when the British launched their attack they found Washington and his men ready. Without the intelligence it received from Mrs. Darragh, the Continental army, instead of forcing the British troops to return to Philadelphia, would almost certainly have been decimated.

LIFE ON THE EDGE
Remarkable Daredevils

Annie Taylor

Few people know that the first person to go over Niagara Falls in a barrel and live was a woman. Annie Taylor, a forty-three-year-old teacher from Michigan who couldn't swim, pulled off the stunt in October of 1901. There were a good many tourists in the area at that time for the Pan American Exposition, and Taylor's heavily promoted dive was a hot ticket. Yet the main event almost didn't happen; the local coroner showed up at the last minute and tried to persuade Taylor not to go over Horseshoe Falls. Her response was a pithy one: "If the authorities stop my attempt, I will jump to my death over the Falls and you will have work for sure." She suffered bruises and some bleeding behind an ear, but no broken bones. Six other people have since attempted the feat (all men); only three have lived to tell the tale.

Maria Speltarini

Like Annie Taylor before her, Speltarini's fame is based on her exploits at Niagara Falls. Unlike Taylor, however, she did not go over the falls in a barrel. In July 1876, Speltarini crossed the Falls on a tightrope. In what was seen as a daring handicap but was probably a deliberate attempt to counteract gusts and lower her center of gravity, she wore thirty-pound weights on each of her ankles.

Lillian Ward

For $150 a day, Ward, known as "the girl without fear," would attempt virtually any stunt Hollywood scriptwriters could think up. As a double for both female and male actors, Ward jumped off cliffs, crashed automobiles, threw herself from the tops buildings, and tumbled down staircases. In the classic *The Perils of Pauline,* it was Ward who played the young woman tied to the railroad tracks by the evil villain.

Lillian Leitzel

This internationally famous high-wire and suspension stunt performer could perform over 200 aerial plunges in one continuous cycle. (She could also do forty revolutions in a row using only one hand.)

ANNIE TAYLOR

Lorena Caven

In the 1930s, this young rider drew huge crowds when she dove into the ocean from high piers astride a specially trained horse. Caven made a career out of her unique skill and had, not surprisingly, few competitors in her field. The intrepid horse was trained by means of a series of jumps into a pool fifteen feet deep.

LIGHTS, CAMERA . . .
Trailblazers in Hollywood

Alice Guy-Blache
This French director was responsible for a short entitled *La Fee aux Choux* (The Cabbage Fairy). Released in 1896, it is believed to be the first fiction film in history.

Dorothy Arzner
Most people, when asked to name a major female director working in Hollywood in the 1930s, would have a hard time coming up with a response. There is only one correct answer: Dorothy Arzner, who started out as a script typist for Paramount, then worked her way up to film editor (she both shot and cut some of the famous bullfighting scenes in Rudolph Valentino's *Blood and Sand*), and eventually worked with such stars as Katherine Hepburn and Clara Bow. Her career is one that turns the starlet's cliché of being "discovered" in a Southern California diner on its head. Arzner was the one who did the discovering: She got her start by making contacts with the many people in the movie industry who frequented her father's restaurant in Hollywood.

Anita Loos
In 1916, Loos could add the title inventor to her long list of professions. Aside from being an actress, screenwriter, novelist and newswriter, Loos is credited with having created the first dialogue titles for the silent films. Her 1925 novel, *Gentlemen Prefer Blondes*, written during her retirement, is currently in its 85th

edition; it was made into both a stage musical and a classic film staring Marilyn Monroe and Jane Russell.

Lotte Reiniger

This German filmmaker was a pioneer in animation. She has been credited with making the first full-length animated film, *The Adventures of Prince Achmed*, with her husband Carl Koch. Her career spanned over seven decades of filmmaking in several countries.

ANITA LOOS

THE LONG ARM OF THE LAW
Women in Law Enforcement and Penology

Esther Hobart Morris

Morris, an accomplished nurse, was the first woman Justice of the Peace in the United States, and she was a very tough customer. Nearly six feet tall and weighing about two hundred pounds, she made quite an imposing impression on the residents of South Pass City (then the largest city in Wyoming) who brought their complaints before her. Not one of her decisions was overturned—not even the assault and battery charge and fine she handed out to her husband. It was Morris who first floated the idea of Wyoming women winning the right to vote at a tea party for legislative candidates in her own home in 1869 (see *Paving the Way for Democracy*, page 98–99). No women anywhere in the world had the right at the time.

Alice Stebbins Wells

Wells was the first policewoman in the United States; she was sworn in as one of Los Angeles's finest on September 12, 1910. Wells faced a unique challenge to her authority; people were constantly accusing her of misusing "her husband's badge." The authorities solved that by issuing her a new model that read "Police Woman's Badge #1" in large, unambiguous letters.

Mary Belle Harris

Before she became one of the country's most highly regarded prison administrators, Harris was a teacher and scholar in Rome. When she returned to her native United States in 1914, she was offered the position of deputy warden at the dreaded Blackwell Island Workhouse in New York. With no prior experience in the field, she set out on a remarkable career as a warden of younger female inmates. Her commitment was to help her prisoners "build within them a wall of self-respect," and in large measure she succeeded. Her facilities were marked by an emphasis on autonomy and independence; Harris made a point of granting inmates a measure of responsibility in the operation of prison facilities. The approach yielded impressive results, and she became known as something of a miracle worker when it came to dealing with difficult inmates. Harris served as superintendent of the model Alderson, West Virginia, women's prison from 1928 to 1941.

ESTHER HOBART MORRIS

Mabel Willebrandt

Assistant attorney general of the United States from 1921 to 1929, she was a scourge to bootleggers during the Prohibition era. Under Willebrandt's direction, the Department of Justice nailed Savannah's Big Four operation, believed to be the largest bootlegging ring in the United States, as well as notorious Cincinnati runner George Remus. In one year, Willebrandt's division (responsible for the Justice Department's tax, prohibition, and prison activities) brought nearly 49,000 cases to court and achieved over 39,000 convictions. Judge John J. Sirica, of Watergate fame, once observed that "if Mabel had worn trousers, she could have been President."

MADAME PRESIDENT . . . AND OTHERS
Women and the Presidency

Belva Lockwood
Lockwood, who was nominated for president twice on the National Equal Rights ticket, was the guiding force behind a landmark bill that mandated equal pay for male and female civil servants performing the same work. She was the first woman to argue a case before the Supreme Court, and she was the person most responsible for women's suffrage being granted in the states of New Mexico, Oklahoma, and Arizona.

Edith Wilson
Someday, many people feel, the United States will have a female president. What these people may not know is that between 1919 and 1921, we had one . . . or at least came close. When Woodrow Wilson suffered a debilitating stroke in the fall of 1919, there was no Twenty-fifth Amendment to the Constitution, and thus no clear direction on who should assume power in the case of a severely incapacitated—but still living—chief executive. Lacking any such formal dictates, First Lady Edith Wilson (who also happened to be the first presidential spouse to claim some Native American blood) took unto herself the sole authority to determine "what the President says." For eighteen months, she controlled all access to the President, reviewed his correspondence, and almost certainly forged his signature on documents requiring presidential approval. Although the First Lady heatedly denied assuming any decision-making capacity, those petitioning the President knew better: they

began addressing their correspondence "Dear Mrs. Wilson." Scholars continue to debate Edith Wilson's role in the Administration's final year and a half, but this much is certain: she had complete control over Wilson and who saw him; she held independent meetings with cabinet members; she kept much later hours than the President, working long into the night as he slept; and she had the final draft approval on the Administration's annual message to the newly convened Congress in 1919. Furthermore, the long list of decisions postponed, undelegated, or completely ignored suggests that a new, untested leader—not a committee or a "shadow president" from the Cabinet—was running the country.

BELVA LOCKWOOD

Jean Westwood

When she was named as co-chair of the 1972 McGovern campaign, Westwood became the first woman to head a major national presidential bid. She was, at the same time, head of the Democratic National Committee. Westwood was an influential party reformer who played a key role in extending opportunities in the Democratic Party to women and minorities.

Anne Armstrong

Armstrong, the first female co-chair of the Republican National Committee, made a dramatic move in 1974: she resigned her post, demanding the resignation of President Richard Nixon upon reviewing the published transcripts of Nixon's Watergate Tapes. She was one of the first high-level Washington Republicans to call on Nixon to step down.

MAKING A CASE FOR EQUALITY
Notable Women in Legal History

Caroline Sheridan Norton

The granddaughter of legendary English dramatist Richard Brinsley Sheridan married a politically powerful MP and barrister, George Norton, in 1827. The couple hit on hard times together, however, and once Caroline had established the beginnings of a literary career of her own, their marriage began to deteriorate. There were some ugly public legal battles, battles Caroline was not likely to win due to the status—or, more accurately, non-status—of women under English law at the time. Nevertheless, she published the highly influential pamphlet *A Plain Letter*, which was a factor not only in the passage of the Infant Custody Bill in 1839 but in her own struggle to obtain legal custody of her children. She won.

Elizabeth Packard

A husband grows tired of his wife and decides that, rather than go to the trouble of divorcing her, he'll simply have her declared insane and placed in a mental hospital for a few years. Such situations were common, accepted by the medical establishment, and completely legal in parts of the United States until Elizabeth Packard contested her confinement to the Jacksonville (Illinois) State Hospital. In a landmark case, she was declared sane in 1864; her husband was prevented from having her recommitted. Her case drew intense of national publicity, helped in the reform of existing laws, and started Packard on a career as an activist.

Arabella Babb Mansfield

When Mansfield was admitted to the Iowa bar on June 15, 1869, she became the first female lawyer in American history. She had studied privately for two years at a local law office. She did not practice, deciding instead to focus her career on teaching at Iowa Wesleyan and DePauw University.

Chicago Joe

This Montana dance hall operator was arrested in 1886 for operating a "hurdy-gurdy house," a genteel euphemism of the day for a brothel. (The hurdy-gurdy was a simple musical instrument then popular in seedier areas of town.) She defended herself in court, arguing that all the music in her establishment was provided by piano, cornet, and violin—without a hurdy-gurdy in sight. She was acquitted.

CHICAGO JOE

Clara Shortridge Foltz

Foltz and her friend Laura de Force Gordon prevailed upon California legislators to change existing laws prohibiting all but white males from practicing law. When the lawmakers obliged, Foltz was able to become the state's first practicing female attorney in 1878. Foltz was one of California's most able and celebrated lawyers, winning case after case and earning the nickname "Portia of the Pacific." One male attorney opposing her once suggested that she should be at home raising children, to which Foltz replied, "A woman had better be in almost any business than raising such men as you."

MAPPING THE HEAVENS
Women in Astronomy

Caroline Herschel

Her elder brother William essentially made this German homemaker his apprentice for his astronomical studies in England in the late 1700s. The two maintained a working relationship that extended over a half century and eventually saw Caroline publish several exhaustively detailed guides under her own name. William discovered the planet we know as Uranus and was appointed Astronomer Royal; for her part, Caroline is credited with discovering eight comets and fourteen nebulae. She received a gold medal from the Royal Astronomical Society in 1828. Caroline, who outlived her brother by 26 years, maintained her scrupulously organized routine of monitoring the heavens well into old age.

Antonia Caetana De Paiva Pereira Maury

After graduating with honors in astronomy from Harvard, Maury began work as an assistant at the school's observatory. She was more interested in revising the classification methods of her superiors than in following set instructions, however. The observatory director, Professor E.C. Pickering, found the system he had personally developed under attack as illogical from the unconventional Maury, whom he seems to have viewed with disdain. (There are indications Pickering made slowing her career something of a pet project.) The victim of soured political relationships, Maury left the school in 1896 in favor of Cornell. The system she had proposed and published in 1897, however, ended up being immensely important in the discovery by Ejnar Hertzsprung of Denmark of high-luminosity giant stars. The new approach eventually won Maury the Cannon Prize from the American Astronomical Society, if not the admiration of Professor Pickering. An independent thinker and an iconoclast, Maury was a superb astronomer whose contributions were crucial to the development of theoretical astrophysics. She returned to Harvard in 1918.

Jocelyn Bell Burnell

In 1967, Burnell—a 24-year-old graduate student monitoring a high-powered telescope—noticed an unknown signal from outer space. Her observations later proved instrumental in the discovery of what we now know as pulsars, a discovery for which her immediate supervisor, Anthony Hewish, won the Nobel Prize. Burnell received no such accolade.

CECELIA HELENA
PAYNE-GAPOSHKIN

Cecelia Helena Payne-Gaposhkin

Becoming the first women Professor at Harvard University is no mean feat, but such was the consequence of the enormous contributions Payne-Gaposhkin made to the field of astronomy. She was the first person to confirm that the chemical composition of the stars and our sun were alike. Her further research on the brightness of stars was of immense importance in later research on the evolution of stars and the configuration of the Milky Way Galaxy.

MEDICINE WOMEN
Females in Medicine
Through the Centuries

Agnodice

Agnodice, who lived in the fourth century B.C., posed as a man in order to attend the lectures of the physician Herophilus and to practice her specialty: gynecology. She achieved a good deal of fame for her competence in the new field and earned the enmity of other doctors. A trumped-up charge of corrupting the morals of women was brought against her, and in order to save her life she revealed her true gender in court. She was then charged with practicing a profession limited by law to men—and acquitted.

Jacqueline Felicie de Almania

De Almania was prosecuted for practicing medicine without a license in 1322 in Paris; witnesses appeared in her defense to testify to her status as the most accomplished surgeon in the city. She made an eloquent plea for the necessity of female doctors, pointing out that many female patients of the day literally preferred to die rather than undergo examination by males. She was nevertheless fined and ordered to abandon her practice, an edict she may well have simply ignored.

Elizabeth Blackwell

The British-born Blackwell decided to embark on a career as a physician when a female friend described her discomfort at having to be examined by a male doctor. Her plans were not an instant success, however: Blackwell was rejected by 29

American medical schools before she was finally accepted at New York's Geneva College in 1847. Upon completing her studies and her residency, she became the first female physician in American history. She was beset by waves of derisive publicity, but finally established a practice in New York City in 1851. Her one-room clinic eventually became the New York Infirmary for Women and Children, which is still in operation today. Blackwell's pioneering experience was instrumental in the establishment of women's medical colleges in the United States.

ELIZABETH BLACKWELL

Ethel Collins Dunham

A trailblazing pediatrician specializing in the care and treatment of premature infants, she helped author standards of care for babies born before term that became the basis for determining accepted practice in the field. (As late as 1935, most hospitals had treated premature babies no differently from other newborns.) Her 1948 book *Premature Infants: A Manual for Physicians*, which relied heavily on her own clinical experience and statistical studies, was another landmark effort. Dunham, who shared a home for nearly fifty years with her close colleague and former classmate, Dr. Martha May Elliot, was the first researcher to isolate prematurity as the single most likely factor to lead to infant death. In 1957, Dr. Dunham was awarded the Howland Medal, the American Pediatric Society's highest honor.

MY BODY, MY DESTINY
Pioneers in the Struggle for Reproductive Rights

Aletta Jacobs
This Dutch woman was the first qualified female doctor in her country's history. In 1882, she founded the world's first contraceptive clinic in Amsterdam in the face of intense opposition from the male-dominated medical establishment there.

Margaret Sanger
Sanger coined the term "birth control" in 1913 in her monthly newsletter *The Woman Rebel*. The frank publication led to her indictment for distributing obscene materials, and she fled to Europe, returning when the indictment was dismissed. She opened a birth control clinic in New York City in 1916 and was arrested in short order. She spent a month in prison but emerged as intent as ever on raising the level of public knowledge about contraception. She began publishing *The Birth Control Review*, which served as the voice of her new movement. Birth control centers began to appear in more and more communities; in 1946, with her ideas no longer a cause for her imprisonment (though far from universally accepted), she helped to found the International Planned Parenthood Federation.

Mary Dennett
A pioneer in the early movement for women's reproductive rights, Dennett formed the National Birth Control League in 1915, the country's first organization to lobby

for liberalization of birth control laws. Dennett also was an early challenger of obscenity laws. When her articles on sex education were deemed obscene in 1922, she continued to distribute them anyway, incurring hefty fines in the process. (Her conviction was later overturned.)

Marie Stopes

MARIE STOPES

Her early life brims with remarkable academic achievements—she was the first female member of the science faculty at Manchester University—but it is as a campaigner for birth control rights in the 1920s that Marie Stopes earned fame. She earned her share of enemies, as well: the medical establishment, the Catholic Church, and even the House of Lords arrayed themselves against her efforts. Stopes's emphasis on birth control as a component of sexual fulfillment was remarkable for the day; few people were willing to publicly advocate that women should be freed from the fear of pregnancy in order to live more complete sexual lives. She was, in a word, revolutionary—and intentionally so. Her countless legal battles brought massive publicity to her cause, although much of it was negative; she was accused by public health officials of committing a "monstrous crime" against society. Stopes's books on contraceptive techniques, at first suppressed on the grounds of obscenity, eventually sold spectacularly.

A NATION OF MANY CULTURES
Beyond the Politics of Hatred and Dissension

Catherine Coffin

Together with her husband Levi, Catherine worked as an early "conductor" on the historic Underground Railroad made famous by the legendary Harriet Tubman. The railroad helped slaves escape from the South by means of a series of clandestine hiding-stations in abolitionist households. Devout Quakers, the Coffins had the distinction of helping to freedom a slave girl named Eliza who was later immortalized as the heroine in Harriet Beecher Stowe's *Uncle Tom's Cabin*. (The Coffins appeared as well, though their names were changed to Halliday.) The Coffins helped more than two thousand slaves cross the border to freedom in Canada.

Emma Lazarus

An accomplished poet, dramatist, and translator, Lazarus's book Songs of a Semite defended ethnic Judaism in a world less sensitive to cultural diversity than ours. Her sonnet, "The New Collosus," five lines of which are reproduced on the Statue of Liberty, hailed the "huddled masses yearning to breathe free" of foreign lands— and earned the sentiment, if not always its author, a place in American popular mythology.

Jessie Daniel Ames

Ames, a white woman, was a leading figure in the founding of the Association of Southern Women for the Prevention of Lynching (ASWPL). This group took as its aim the organization of the wives and mothers of white male southerners most likely to engage in lynching. The ASWPL was a powerful moral force that some historians feel actually led to a reduction in lynching incidents in the South. Although the ASWPL was not out to change the underlying framework of race relations in the South, it was an impressive grass-roots reaction to hate crimes and assaults typically justified in the name of protecting "virtuous Southern woman-hood."

ELIZABETH ECKFORD

Joanne Robinson

In 1955, Robinson was head of the Local Women's Political Council in Montgomery, Alabama. She got word of a courageous local woman named Rosa Parks who had refused a conductor's request to move to the rear of a city bus and was now in jail. Robinson saw the opportunity to put into action her group's long-discussed plans for a boycott of the city's bus system. She and two students made a clandestine nighttime trip to Alabama State College, where they used duplicating equipment to print thousands of notices advocating a boycott. The notices showed up everywhere; the historic boycott was on.

Elizabeth Eckford and MinnieJean Brown

These courageous young women, fifteen and sixteen years old, respectively, faced down the segregationist Arkansas state government (not to mention violent mobs and hostile schoolmates) in seeking admission to Little Rock High in 1957. The girls were two of the nine brave black students around whom the first great national crisis of the civil rights movement swirled. Federal troops were called in by the Eisenhower administration to protect them.

NO BUSINESS LIKE SHOW BUSINESS
Memorable Vaudeville Performers

Lola Montez

Her notorious "spider dance" won her the ecstatic adulation of thousands of men, among whom were numbered a Polish prince, Ludwig, King of Bavaria, and Franz Liszt. Montez, who may or may not have been linked to European nobility, cultivated an air of eccentricity and enjoyed a brief but unrivaled period of stardom in the western United States. In her heyday, she delighted in breaking the rules laid down for "common women": she smoked cigars, elbowed her way into poker games, and played a mean game of tenpins. When she was ridiculed onstage by another performer, however, she left San Francisco, the scene of her greatest triumphs. Her attempt to transplant her act to California's small mining towns failed, and she relocated to Australia, where her act was well received. On her return to the U.S., she attempted several comebacks, but her career was never the same.

Adah Isaacs Menken

Menken was most remarkable not for her melodramatic acting and scantily-clad attempts at spectacle, but for her shrewd public relations and media savvy. She was an expert marketer of her primary product (herself), and she was not afraid to create controversy to draw a crowd. (She once sported a huge Confederate flag in her hotel room during a Civil War tour through pro-Union California; the papers ate it up.) Her posters and stage shows were calculated to titillate her almost exclusively male audience, but her real genius lay in charming newspaper reviewers. She conquered a notoriously tough array of Virginia City critics that included Mark Twain, whose glowing account of her performance was reprinted nationwide. She was a legend—and a calculating purveyor of scandal—on the West Coast for years. Menken was the Madonna, as it were, of the gold rush.

EFFIE CHERRY

Elizabeth, Effie, Jessie, and Addie Cherry

Why was there an act known as the Cherry Sisters on the vaudeville circuit in the 1890s? The answer is complicated. From time to time in American popular entertainment the public becomes fascinated with pure, unadulterated talentlessness. Audiences paid good money to see this wretchedly off-key sister group, which appeared behind a wire screen designed to protect the performers from the hail of garbage that traditionally accompanied their performances. The act drew gleeful, derisive audiences in spite of (or perhaps because of) less-than-glowing critical assessments from the press. "It is sincerely hoped," *The New York Times* intoned solemnly, "that nothing like them will ever be seen again." There are enough instances of contrived, intentionally terrible press about the Cherry sisters that one wonders whether the sisters were a little brighter than contemporary accounts give them credit for being. After all, the act—wire screen and all—did play for years.

ON OUR OWN AND MANAGING NICELY, THANK YOU

Enterprising Women Who Broke New Ground

Therese Coincoin This former slave was the long-time concubine of a Frenchman named Claude Metoyer who purchased her freedom for her. When the two parted—apparently amicably—in 1786, he deeded her a great deal of prime Louisiana land. Coincoin took to agricultural life with a vengeance, raising corn, cotton, and tobacco and managing a good number of cattle as well. The estate she developed from scratch was quite profitable, and enabled her not only to purchase the freedom of her children but to leave them a substantial inheritance as well.

Reindeer Mary The list of prominent, successful turn-of-the-century female Eskimo entrepreneurs is, it is safe to say, probably a comparatively short one. In fact, it may well contain only one name, that of Reindeer Mary—founder of a huge business that dealt in reindeer meat and by-products. The operation, which she managed on her own, was located near Point Barrow, Alaska.

Rebecca Pennock Lukens She was thirty-one-years-old and pregnant when her husband died in 1825. He asked her to take responsibility for the Brandywine Iron Works he had struggled with for so long; she complied. Less than a decade after taking over the firm's operations, she had paid off all her husband's debts and turned the ill-managed concern into a profitable enterprise. Lukens quickly became the most prominent citizen in town; if there were other female industrialists in the United States in the early nineteenth century, let alone any who achieved such levels of success, we have seen no record of them. She died a wealthy woman in 1854. Five years later the company name was changed to the Lukens Steel Company.

REBECCA PENNOCK LUKENS

Patty Smith Hill, Mildred Hill, and Jessica M. Hill

Women songwriters were in short supply in 1893, but in that year the Hill sisters composed a little number known as "Happy Birthday to You." It became a cultural standard and, eventually, the most popular copyrighted song in the English language. Contrary to popular belief, the song is not in the public domain and will continue to earn royalties until the year 2010. The Hills' composition currently earns over $1 million per year in royalties; every play, movie, or programmable watch that uses the tune must pay a fee. Warner Communications paid $25 million for the rights in 1988.

Sarah Haldeman

When her husband died in 1905, she assumed control of the Girard State Bank. Under her leadership, it was kept on a steady course and commended two years later as "one of the most solid financially in the state" by a local business reporter.

ON THE BEAT
Reporters Who Flouted Convention to Get a Story

Mary Livermore

Reporters of either sex were more than a little nervous at Abraham Lincoln's inauguration in 1860—rumors were flying that an assassination attempt would take place before the man from Illinois could take the oath of office. But Livermore—the only woman present at the proceedings—got the story without incident. She later did mountains of relief work on the battlefield for Union soldiers, founded an influential suffragist newspaper, campaigned tirelessly for women's rights, and edited, with Frances Willard, an exhaustive survey of notable women of the nineteenth century.

Nellie Bly

Her real name was Elizabeth Cochrane Seaman, but it was under the pen name of Nellie Bly that she exposed the inhumane conditions at the notorious Blackwell's Island women's asylum in 1887. (She had to feign insanity to do so.) Later, she met (and beat) the fictional Phileas Fogg's feat of traversing the globe in 80 days; her *Around the World in 72 Days* described her real-life journeys by steamboat, rickshaw, railroad, and even sampan.

Winifred Sweet Black Bonfils

Also known as Annie Laurie, this Hearst-employed investigative reporter was known for using ingenious means to nail down a story. Discouraged while trying to get the scoop on the tidal wave that pummeled Galveston, Texas in 1900, Bonfils disguised herself as a boy to slip through police lines. She also served as a reporter in Europe during World War I, and is believed to have been the first woman in history to cover a boxing match.

Martha Gellhorn

MARTHA GELLHORN

Gellhorn was of that rare breed, the female battlefield news correspondent. She was the only woman to cover the Russian bombing of Helsinki, and she filed remarkable first-hand reports of both the Spanish Civil War and the Nazi occupation of Czechoslovakia in 1939. She balanced compelling accounts of the suffering of war victims with incisive interviews with world leaders. Her pieces in *Collier's* magazine were among the most widely read of the period. Gellhorn's intrusion on what had been (and, to a large degree, still remains) an exclusively male beat was facilitated to some degree by her marital status. Her husband and fellow writer was another world traveler by the name of Ernest Hemingway.

ON THE FRONTIER
Women Whose Lives Bridged
Native American and White Society

Sacagawea

She was born in what would later become either western Montana or Eastern Idaho sometime around 1784; in late 1800, this Shoshone woman was kidnaped by a band of Minnetaree who eventually traded her to a French trapper. She eventually served as guide, interpreter, and envoy for Lewis and Clark on their legendary expedition. Her aid in selecting the most direct routes and in securing horses for the explorers to use in crossing the Rocky Mountains was essential to the success of the mission.

Frances Slocum/Maconaqua

Nineteenth-century book publishers could count on one sure formula for a bestseller: the dramatic (and often embellished) first-hand accounts of white frontier women kidnaped by "Indian savages" and later returned to white society. While such accounts sold briskly, they did not tell the whole story of the cultural encounters between whites and Indians. Frances Slocum's experience, for instance— by no means the only one of its kind— was different. She was abducted during a raid by Delaware tribesmen on her home in Wilkes-Barre, Pennsylvania in 1778. Slocum somehow ended up with a tribe of Miami Indians, took the name Maconaqua ("Little Bear"), and was accepted as a member of the community. She married a chief in the village, raised two sons, and oversaw one hundred head of livestock in the prosperous village in which she had settled. Fifty-nine years after her abduction, she was located by joyous family members who expected her to return to her white origins. Instead, they came face-to-face with a smiling, gray-haired woman high in the village social order who had forgotten how to speak English and refused to return east with them. Slocum/Maconaqua died in 1847.

Bright Eyes/Susette LaFlesche Tibbles

As translator for Chief Standing Bear of Nebraska's Ponca Tribe, Bright Eyes (whose Western name was Susette LaFlesche Tibbles) traveled the United

SACAGAWEA

States in an attempt to bring to light the injustice of government policies toward Native American tribes. Later, she came into her own as a lecturer and aided in the passage of the Dawes Severalty Act of 1887, which granted full citizenship rights to American Indians.

ON THE FRONT LINES
Women Who Distinguished Themselves
in Wartime

Manto Mavrogenous

To say that Mavrogenous believed in Greek independence from Turkey is something of an understatement. When the Greek revolution against Turkey began in 1821, she raised, at her own expense, a private army of guerrilla fighters whom she personally led to victory in a number of bloody campaigns. She also supplied Greece with naval protection against pirates by purchasing and outfitting two ships to protect the vulnerable islands. She was awarded the rank of lieutenant general.

Belle Reynolds

Reynolds, whose husband William was a lieutenant with the Union Army, had traveled with the 17th Illinois Infantry Encampment for nine months when it reached Tennessee in the spring of 1862. On April 6, the troops came under heavy Confederate fire in what would later be known as the Battle of Shiloh, the first great western battle of the war. For a full week Reynolds dodged bullets and cannonballs, assisted surgeons in caring for the hundreds of Union casualties, and served as an armed guard on hospital boats. She was awarded the commission of major on the spot by the Governor of Illinois, who had boarded a supply steamer to visit the battlefield site.

Mary Lindell

Lindell used family connections to secure a position as a nurse on the Western Front in 1914; she remained there for four years and earned a Croix de Guerre for her courage under fire. She once evacuated a field station under heavy enemy shelling—and was then erroneously reported dead by the London *Daily Mail*. During the Second World War, at age 45, she organized an escape line for the French Resistance. She was captured by the Germans twice, and on the second occasion, knowing that death awaited her, she attempted to escape her captors by leaping off a speeding train. She was shot and seriously injured in the attempt, and she did not escape. Even-

BELLE REYNOLDS

tually she was transferred to a concentration camp, where she was once again falsely reported to have died. Severely stricken with pneumonia, she engineered her own release and that of the other British captives in the camp as part of a hostage release program camp officials had agreed to with the Swedish Red Cross.

Lieutenant Jane A. Lombardi

When her air base in Danang came under enemy fire in 1968, Lt. Lombardi acted quickly and decisively in evacuating dozens of sick and wounded from the facility. She was eventually awarded the Air Force Bronze Star, thereby becoming the first combat-decorated female in American history.

ON THE JOB
Women Who Fought for a Better Workplace

Rose Schneiderman

At thirteen, she left her job as a clerk in a department store to earn better pay as a machine operator. Within five years, she and a coworker had founded the first local of the United Cloth Hat and Cap Makers Union. By 1918, she had become president of the Women's Trade Union League. Schneiderman was a personal participant in every major strike in the textile industry in the first two decades of the century, and was a legendary early organizer of working women.

Mother Jones

This legendary activist, whose career extended over the better part of a century, was a thorn in the side of the American political establishment for so long that she eventually became a symbol for tireless progressivism. In the early part of this century, she put a human face on the routinely ignored abuses of child laborers by marching scores of young coal miners from their Pennsylvania mines to the exclusive Oyster Bay residence of Teddy Roosevelt. Such explosive media demonstrations were instrumental in heightening public concern over the issue; stringent national child labor laws were eventually passed.

Florence Kelley

Kelley was a fierce lobbyist for legislation limiting the number of hours of work an employer could demand from female employees, and for minimum-wage laws for women. These were radical concepts in the 1890s and 1900s, when female workers were often forced to spend twelve hours a day standing in the same place. As executive secretary of the Consumers League, Kelley attempted to establish a system of labels identifying conscientious manufacturers who maintained protective work policies for women and children. Her emphasis on female workers as a class of employees worthy of formal protection under the law brought her into conflict with a later generation of feminists seeking equal protection for all citizens, regardless of sex.

MOTHER JONES

Iris Rivera

Rivera, a Chicago legal secretary, lost her job in 1977 because she refused to make coffee for her employer. Her rationale: "(1) I don't drink coffee, (2) it's not listed as one of my job duties, and (3) ordering the secretaries to fix the coffee is taking the role of homemaker too far." Although she was not rehired, her case resulted in a large-scale protest by Chicago secretaries and generated considerable network news coverage. The activist group Women Employed presented Rivera's boss with a "coffee demerit badge": a bag of soggy coffee grounds.

OVERCOMING THE ODDS
Women Winning with Persistence and Dedication

Victorine LeFourcade

Born to a wealthy family in the late 1700s, LeFourcade fell in love with a young journalist of scant means, Julius Bossuet. Her parents pressured her to wed a banker named Renelle; she did this, but Renelle treated her so cruelly that, after several years of discontent, she faked her own death—or, if you take the records of the time at face value, came back to life after her lover Bossuet happened to visit the gravesite and opened her coffin for a final look. In any event, because she was thought to be dead, Victorine was free to begin a new life with Bossuet. The two escaped to America, where they lived in happiness for two decades. When they returned to France, Renelle apparently caught wind of the scheme and had his wife put under arrest. Victorine, however, had attained her goal; the courts would not force her to return to her first husband.

Abigail Duniway

In 1871, Duniway founded a weekly Portland, Oregon newspaper known as the *New Northwest*. This marked the beginning of a long career of writings and lectures aimed at winning women the right to vote. In 1883, she managed to persuade the state legislature to authorize a constitutional amendment granting female suffrage, but the measure required approval as a ballot proposition, and Oregonian men voted it down. A similar measure was defeated in 1900. Duniway got a women's suffrage proposal on the ballot in 1908, only to see it, too, go down to defeat. In 1910, she mounted her final campaign—and lost by the largest margin yet. At long last, in 1912, an enfranchisement measure that the ailing, seventy-eight-year-old Duniway had not sponsored or campaigned for passed by a scant four thousand votes. At the next election, Duniway became the first Oregonian woman to cast a legal ballot. (The Nineteenth Amendment to the Constitution, granting women voting rights nationwide, would not pass until 1920.)

MYRA BRADWELL

Myra Bradwell

In 1868, with the encouragement of her husband James, a prominent attorney, Myra Bradwell began publishing the weekly *Chicago Legal News*. The paper, which covered legal developments throughout the United States, was an instant success, as was the legal forms business Myra also headed. Mrs. Bradwell's unfailingly accurate renderings of current Illinois statutes were always the first widely available editions of the law after the Illinois legislature adjourned; the early reprints were one of the reasons her paper quickly became the single-most-influential legal publication west of the Alleghenies. In the Great Chicago Fire of 1871, the paper's offices were completely destroyed. The only thing the Bradwells managed to rescue was the list of subscribers, but that was enough for Myra. After her family had been safely relocated, she boarded a train for Milwaukee and resumed work on the paper. The next issue of the *Chicago Legal News* was published three days later—right on schedule. It continued in this fashion for the duration of her tenure as editor.

PATENTLY INGENIOUS
Notable Female Inventors and Designers

Gertrude A. Muller
An early children's products entrepreneur, Muller founded the Juvenile Wood Products Company in 1924. Her firm flourished through the Great Depression. She is credited with developing, among many other inventions, the first child car seat. For her pioneering emphasis on the safety of her company's products (she was one of the first to conduct auto crash studies), she was named National Veteran of Safety by the National Safety Council and invited to the 1954 White House Conference on Highway Safety. She served as president of the successful firm she had founded until her death in 1954.

Margaret Knight
Knight, one of the more versatile inventors of either sex for the five decades before her death in 1914, had little formal schooling. She was granted at least twenty-seven and possibly as many as eighty-seven patents for such diverse items as shoe-cutting machines, window frames, rotary engines, and sequential numbering devices. Her most lucrative patent was probably the one she was granted for the development of the square-bottomed paper bag in 1871.

Mary Dixon Kies
In 1809, Kies, a Connecticut mother and homemaker, became the first woman in American history to receive a patent. Her weaving machine was initially well received, but not the huge commercial success her family had hoped it would be.

She did, however, receive a personal note of congratulations from Dolley Madison.

Hannah Slater

Slater, the wife of a Rhode Island mill founder, revolutionized the textile industry in the early 19th century. Noticing the weakness of the traditional flax threads used for sewing, Slater introduced the hardier cotton thread. Cloth production was never the same.

Mary Engle Pennington

Chief among Pennington's many accomplishments in the dawning field of large-scale food storage, handling, and transport was her leading role in the

GERTRUDE A. MULLER

development of refrigerated railroad cars in 1917. The standards she authored as part of her work in support of government supply efforts during World War I stood for nearly three decades. Her accomplishments in the perishable products division of the United States Food Administration won her a Notable Service Medal. Her career in perishable food transport field was wide-ranging and innovative; she was the first woman accepted as a member of the American Society of Refrigerating Engineers.

Teresa and Mary Thompson

In 1960, the Thompson sisters, eight and nine years old, respectively, invented a solar tepee as part of a competition in a school science fair. They later received a patent on the invention they called the "Wigwarm." The Thompsons are believed to be the youngest Americans ever granted a patent.

PATRIOTIC MUSIC
Women Who Played
Key Roles in the Composition of
Our National Songs

Mary Young Pickersgill

There wouldn't have been a Star-Spangled Banner if there had not first been a star-spangled banner. A year before Francis Scott Key composed what would later become America's national anthem, the commandant at Fort McHenry in Maryland commissioned Mary Young Pickersgill to create a flag "so large that the British will have no difficulty seeing it from a distance." Pickersgill was no newcomer to the business of flagmaking; she learned the craft from her mother, who had made the first flag of the American Revolution. After six weeks of work, she presented a massive flag 36 feet high and 42 feet wide. The flag that inspired Key hangs today in the Smithsonian Institution in Washington, D.C.

Julia Ward Howe

Howe, who wrote the text to *The Battle Hymn of the Republic*, after visiting an encampment of the Union army, received only $4 in compensation from the *Atlantic* when her work was published. The song, whose tune is that of *John Brown's Body*, became the Union anthem during the Civil War.

Katharine Lee Bates

Bates, an English professor, scaled Pikes Peak in Colorado during an 1893 summer trip to the western states. She was so inspired by the dazzling view from the summit of the 14,110-foot crest that she wrote what would become *America the Beautiful*. "It was then and there," she wrote later, "as I was looking out over the sea-like expanse of fertile country spreading away so far under those ample skies, that the opening lines of the hymn floated into my mind."

JULIA WARD HOWE

PAVING THE WAY TO DEMOCRACY
The First Women to Vote

Mary Jarrett White

White voted in Georgia's spring 1920 elections even though the Nineteenth Amendment did not become the law of the land until August of that year. To this day, no one is quite sure how she got away with it. The records show that she was legally registered to vote in late 1919, but they do not indicate what means she used to persuade officials to list her on the rolls of those eligible to cast a ballot. But women had voted before in the U.S., on the state and territorial level, as demonstrated by . . .

Louisa Ann Swain

Wyoming's women were the first in any state or territory to gain the legal right to vote; the frontier territory's extension of the suffrage to women in 1870 predated the nationwide adoption of the Nineteenth Amendment by fifty years. The first woman to take advantage of the new state of affairs was Louisa Ann Swain of Laramie, who went to the polls early on the morning of September 6, 1870. Swain thus became the first woman to cast a *legal* vote in American history. But she was, in a sense, beaten to the punch by . . .

Charlotte "Charley" Parkhurst

In 1868, Parkhurst, who masqueraded as a male named Charley in carrying out her duties as a California stagecoach driver, became the first woman to cast a ballot in a presidential election. Her vote was illegal, but it was not until her death in 1879 that her gender—and thus her historical status—was discovered. And yet even she was preceded by . . .

LOUISA ANN SWAIN

Anonymous Postrevolutionary New Jersey Women

Shortly after the United States gained independence from Britain, the legislators drafting the state of New Jersey's voting laws left a loophole that allowed women, as well as men, the right to vote. Vote they did—until a close election was perceived as having been decided by ballots cast by females. The loophole was quickly closed up.

PLAY BALL!
Female Ballplayers Honored in the National Baseball Hall of Fame

Note: The players listed below were all standout performers in the All-American Girl's Professional Baseball League, which came into being during World War II and continued play until the mid-fifties. The league was a popular attraction in the Midwest, and although statistics were erratic due to evolving rules and equipment changes, the picture that remains is one of a special group of female athletes playing at a high professional level. An exhibit honoring the league and its players was recently installed permanently at the Hall of Fame in Cooperstown, New York.

Dorothy "Kammie" Kamenshek, 1B
Rockford Peaches, 1943–1953
Former New York Yankee first baseman Wally Pipp said that Kamenshek was "a better fielder than most major leaguers." It was Pipp's opinion that Kamenshek could have been the first woman to play major league baseball. She was a two-time league batting champion and a seven-time All-Star. Kamenshek compiled an excellent lifetime batting mark of .292.

Doris Sams, P-OF
Muskegon/Kalamazoo Lassies, 1946–1953
Sams was named Player of the Year in 1948 and 1949. Like many players in the league she played every day, serving as an outfielder when she wasn't pitching. She

compiled a lifetime batting average of .290 and won the batting championship in 1949.

Jean Faut, P-3B-OF
South Bend Blue Sox, 1946–1951

Faut accomplished a feat unmatched in any major league career: she pitched two perfect games. Her lifetime earned-run average was a microscopic 1.23, a tremendous achievement. She was a four-time All-Star and won 20 games on three occasions.

DOROTHY "KAMMIE"
KAMENSHEK

PRODIGIES
Young, Brilliant, and
Impossible to Pigeonhole

Maria Gaetana Agnesi Proficient at several languages, including Latin, by the age of nine, Agnesi received much attention for her mathematical prowess, even though mathematics was not her first preference. She was the oldest child in a large and wealthy Italian merchant family, but she rejected the lifestyle to which she was born. She would have entered a convent, but her father vetoed the idea. Instead, she entered an agreement with her father that she could live a simple life, be exempt from the social obligations that come with being born to nobility, and be able to attend mass whenever she desired. In return, she would not enter the convent but would devote herself to the study of mathematics. In her 1748 treatise *Foundations of Analysis*, Agnesi combined algebra, analytic geometry, calculus, and differential equations into an orderly arrangement. This made the development of mathematics and mathematical theory clearer and better understood by generations of later students to come. For her contributions, she received honors and gifts from Pope Benedict XIV. Her later life was dedicated to the study of theology and to working with the poor and aged.

Juana de la Cruz At age nine, Juana de la Cruz had already exhibited her extraordinary talents: she had developed acute literary skills and a mastery of Latin. Unfortunately, the educational opportunities open to seventeenth-century women (much less girls) in Mexico did not include universities. So it was that   in 1669 Juana entered a convent, where she compiled a library of more than 4,000 books, wrote poetry and plays, and studied literature and science. Twenty years later, when some of her works were published in Spain, Church officials tried to force Juana to restrict her studies to religious subjects. She was able to withstand the pressure for about two years, but she was finally obliged to give in to the demands.

VINNIE REAM HOXIE

Lucinda Foote Yale University did not admit women until 1969; that was 186 years too late for child prodigy Lucinda Foote, who tried in vain to win entry in 1783. Foote's mental ability so astonished Yale's president, Ezra Stiles, that he gave her, instead of admission and the chance to earn a degree, the following remarkable testimonial: "Let it be known unto you, that I have tested Miss Lucinda Foote, aged 12, by way of examination, proving that she has made laudable progress in the languages of the learned, viz, the Latin and the Greek; to such an extent that I found her translating and expounding with perfick [sic] ease, both words and sentences in the whole of Vergil's Aeneid, in selected orations of Cicero, and in the Greek testament. I testify that were it not for her sex, she would be considered fit to be admitted as a student . . . ."

Vinnie Ream Hoxie The teenaged Hoxie, an accomplished sculptor whose work overshadowed that of many male competitors, was the first woman awarded an artistic commission by the United States Government. By virtue of her work on a statue of Abraham Lincoln near the end of the Civil War in Washington, the young artist was one of the last people to see the President alive. Her memorial to Lincoln was placed in the Capitol rotunda despite a firestorm of criticism surrounding her selection as official sculptor.

THE RIGHT TO LEARN
Refusing to Be Refused an Education

Sofia Vasilevna Kovalevskaia

Born in Moscow in 1850, Kovalevskaia had to concoct a fictitious marriage at the age of eighteen in order to study mathematics: no Russian university would admit women, and all females were prohibited by law from leaving the country without written permission from a father or husband. In Berlin in 1874, she produced not one but three doctoral dissertations to win her degree, as she knew she had to present an air-tight case to become the first woman ever granted a doctorate in mathematics. She won the degree—and the prestigious Prix Bordin fourteen years later. It was only after winning this, the highest honor of the French Academy of Sciences, that she was permitted an academic position in her homeland.

Mary Lyon

When she enrolled at a boarding school in 1817, Mary Lyon was very nearly destitute: she had to weave two blankets and give them to the school in exchange for admission. Twenty years later, Lyon founded Mt. Holyoke Female Seminary, which was the first school of higher education for women in the United States. It offered a revolutionary (for women) curriculum that included history, science, and math—subjects thought by many to be not only inappropriate but physically and mentally hazardous for "members of the fairer sex."

Mary Shadd Cary

Born a free woman in Delaware in 1823, Cary had to travel to Pennsylvania for her education, as her home state refused to offer blacks schooling of any kind. Cary, the first African-American woman to edit a newspaper, founded the *Provincial Freeman* in 1853; her readers were fugitive slaves who had crossed the border into Canada. She eventually earned a law degree from Howard University.

MARY SHADD CARY

Anna Howard Shaw

She entered Boston University's School of Theology in 1876 with one goal: to become a minister. As a woman, she had no access to the financial aid her male classmates enjoyed, but she found preaching assignments outside of the school and was the only member of her class to graduate free from debt. She later earned her M.D. at the same institution.

Cornelia Sorabji

She was the first female student at Decca College in Poona, India; when she graduated at the top of her class, she began preparations to attend a British university using the scholarship money reserved for the number-one student. That money was withdrawn solely on the basis of her gender. Shortly thereafter, Sorabji won a fellowship at a prestigious Indian college, and was eventually the beneficiary of a special decree that enabled her to become the first female in India to practice law.

THE SKY'S THE LIMIT
Women in the Air

Ruth Law
On November 19, 1916, Law flew nonstop from Chicago to Hornell, New York, thereby setting the American nonstop cross-country record for both men and women. The flight took six hours and covered 590 miles, a staggering distance at that time. Law attempted to enlist as a fighter pilot in World War I, but was turned down by no less an authority than Secretary of War Newton D. Baker.

Valeria Ivanovna Khomyakova
A fighter pilot in the Great Patriotic War, as World War II is known in Russia, Khomyakova is recognized as the first woman pilot in history to shoot down an enemy bomber. She brought down a German Junkers-88 in late 1942 in a dogfight over Saratov.

Jacqueline Cochran
Beginning in the 1930s and continuing until 1965, Cochran was a competitor in a dizzying number of international air races; she won the prestigious Bendix transcontinental race in 1934 and later became the first woman to break the sound barrier. Cochran was one of the creators of the Women's Air Service Pilots (W.A.S.P.) group during World War II. She was elected to the U.S. Aviation Hall of Fame in 1971.

Valentina Tereshkova

In 1963, Tereshkova became the first woman space traveler. She orbited the globe 48 times aboard the Soviet craft *Vostok 6*. Her orbit total exceeded that of the six male American astronauts who had accomplished earth orbit to that point. Tereshkova was selected for her history-making flight when Tatyana Tochillova, the first choice as the world's premier woman in space, failed a preflight physical. Once she made her mark on the aerospace world, however, Tereshkova served her country primarily as a celebrity, making many speaking appearances. The Soviet Union, having achieved its public relations coup, would not send another woman into space until 1982. The United States would not launch the space shuttle flight carrying American astronaut Sally Ride until 1983.

VALENTINA TERESHKOVA

SPEAKING OUT
Courageous Women Orators

Mary Lease

Lease, a mother of four who was admitted to the Kansas bar in 1886, was one of the most gifted orators of her day. A first-hand witness to the collapsing farm economy, she was a leading force in the organization of the Populist movement that challenged the two-party system in the prairie states. Her stump speeches attacking both Democrats and Republicans during the elections of 1890 became the stuff of legend. "You farmers were told two years ago to raise a big crop," she would bellow from the platform. "Well, you did—and what became of it? Six-cent corn, ten-cent oats, two-cent beef. We want the accursed foreclosure system wiped out . . . . What you farmers need is to raise less corn and more hell!" Hers was a remarkably effective appeal that helped the Populists catapult to national prominence. Although she herself did not run for office, Lease was probably the first American woman to sway male voters to her cause in large numbers.

Anna Shaw

Shaw, a pioneering suffragist who worked with Susan B. Anthony, was on a westbound train headed toward a voting rights rally at which she was scheduled to speak when a severe snowstorm stopped the locomotive in its tracks. She was the only woman among a group of rowdy male passengers. When the cattlemen and cowboys finally tired of their poker games, one man approached Shaw and sheepishly explained that he recognized her from an earlier lecture. "I've been tellin' the fellers about it," he went on, "and we'd like to have a lecture now." She obliged them, and passed the evening singing hymns and expounding with vigor on the necessity of female suffrage to her unlikely—but extremely polite—audience. At the close of the meeting, the men donated their overcoats to make a comfortable bed for Shaw, on which she slept peacefully until the snowplow arrived the next morning.

Sarah and Angelina Grimke

The sisters, South Carolina natives, were crusading pioneers in the antislavery movement of the nineteenth century. Sarah, the elder sister, broke the law in 1804 when, at the age of twelve, she taught a slave child to read and write. Both Grimke girls

MARY LEASE

were punished. The Grimke sisters, both persuasive orators, were the first Americans to overcome the prevailing edicts against speech on public platforms by women. Even though their audiences were often receptive to their message, the sisters faced boos and catcalls from male audience members who felt women had no place in public debate.

THE SPORTING LIFE
Women Who Outdid Men

Hessie Donahue
If you're ever down on your luck and need some ready cash, find a boxing fan, ask if the fan's ever heard of legendary heavyweight champion John L. Sullivan, and propose a bet: "True or false—the first person ever to knock Sullivan out in a boxing ring was a woman." You'll win. Mrs. Hessie Donahue used to don a loose blouse, bloomers, and boxing gloves and stand in for a few fake rounds with the champ as part of a vaudeville act. One night in 1892, however, Sullivan connected with a genuine blow to Hessie's face—and got her mad. She retaliated with a solid punch of her own and knocked the previously unbested Sullivan out for over a minute.

Jackie Mitchell
Mitchell, the first woman ever to sign a contract with a professional baseball club, was pitching for Chattanooga in an April 1931 exhibition game against the New York Yankees. She faced Babe Ruth and Lou Gehrig, back-to-back—and struck them both out.

Ada Evans Dean
Upon hearing that her jockey had taken ill and could not ride in a 1906 race, horse-owner Dean sped to the track and rode her horse to victory—twice. Afterward, she admitted that she had never ridden in a horse race before.

Conchita Cintron

Cintron, the first female to compete at a high professional level as a bullfighter, mastered over 1,200 bulls. Her career, which began in Lima, Peru when she was only twelve years old, was an uphill struggle, to say the least. She faced many challenges in this intensely male-dominated sport, especially in her goal to appear in the great rings of Europe. (She was eventually successful, although she was once arrested for appearing at a bullfight in France.) Perhaps her most triumphant moment came in her farewell appearance in Spain in 1949. She defied the rules of the ring by entering on horseback, dismounting, executing a textbook-perfect set of maneuvers,

HESSIE DONAHUE

and tossing her sword to the ground, refusing to kill the bull, as was customary. The authorities were outraged, and had her placed under arrest. The crowd cheered so loudly in her favor, however, that she was pardoned for the "transgression." She never appeared in the ring again.

STING ARTISTS
Practitioners of the Less-than-honorable Vocation of Big-time Bluffing

Kate and Margaret Fox

In March of 1848, these Rochester, New York, sisters began the perpetration of an intricate hoax that, for a time, captured the nation's imagination. They lived in a house that was reputed to be haunted; accordingly, the Fox girls, aged twelve and nine, respectively, gave a convincing imitation of poltergeist phenomena for their gullible and superstitious mother. Kate would snap her fingers three times; a mysterious three-knock return would emanate from the walls. The stunts started out simple, but eventually the girls worked out a detailed alphabetic code which they purported to use in communicating with "the other side." Soon the scam took in not only the girls' astonished parents but such luminaries as James Fenimore Cooper, Horace Greeley, and the First Lady of the United States. The girls eventually began a lucrative business offering seances at $100 a sitting; their clandestine special effects became more and more impressive. After forty years of national fame, Margaret confessed that all of the sisters' purported encounters with spiritual entities had been fraudulent.

Constance Cassandra Chadwick

After moving to Cleveland in 1886, this enterprising young women devised a bold scam that enabled her to become a millionaire . . . for a while. Chadwick passed herself off as the mistress of steel magnate Andrew Carnegie and claimed to have given birth to one of his children. She "borrowed" $40 million from a bank that accepted her claim once she convinced a starstruck bank official that Carnegie had deposited over $12 million in securities for her use in the bank's vault. The deposit box she offered as proof, which contained only newspaper articles about Carnegie, was not opened by the banker until Chadwick had left for parts unknown. With her new fortune, Chadwick invested in the stock market and lived a lavish lifestyle for a time, but was wiped out in a market crash. She was brought to trial and convicted in 1870; two years later, she died in prison. It is estimated that, when the dust settled, her massive embezzlement cost the country's banking system over $100 million.

KATE FOX

Therese Humbert

Spinning a tale was always something this young French woman did well; in fact, she once told two stories that were worth 64 million francs. Her first tale involved a rich elderly woman who had left her a fortune and a chateau in her will. The second one involved an American millionaire whose life she saved when he became ill on a train. He supposedly expressed his gratitude by leaving Humbert and her sister $20 million. Therese claimed she would come into the fortune, stored in bonds and securities, when her sister came of age and the necessary legal proceedings were concluded. With this much money coming to her, Humbert was able to live on a series of generous credit lines totaling in the neighborhood of 64 million francs. Eventually, when creditors grew tired of her lame excuses, they opened the safe deposit box in which all her personal documents were purportedly stored. Its contents: a single brick. The episode earned Humbert a three-and-a-half-year jail term.

STRENGTH IN NUMBERS
Important Contributors to Mathematics and Computer Science

Hypatia
Born circa 370 A.D., this daughter of the Director of the University of Alexandria studied in Athens under Plutarch the Younger and Asclepegeneia, and eventually taught geometry, algebra, and astronomy at Alexandria. She designed variations on the astrolabe (an instrument used by sailors to determine the altitude of celestial bodies) and the hydroscope (used to measure the specific gravity of liquids).

Amalie Noether
A *New York Times* article printed after her death in 1935 offered one colleague's assessment of Noether: "(She) was the most significant creative mathematical genius produced since the higher education of women began. In the realm of algebra, in which the most gifted mathematicians have been busy for centuries, she discovered methods which have proved of enormous importance in the development of the present-day younger generation of mathematicians." The colleague: Albert Einstein. For all her brilliance, she was prohibited for much of her career from lecturing openly; at Gottingen University in Germany, she had to teach classes officially designated as being led by a male colleague.

Ada Augusta Byron, Lady Lovelace
Even though she lived in an era of looms and spindles rather than semiconductors,

it is no coincidence that Ada's name is also that of a computer language used by the U.S. Department of Defense. Her natural talent for mathematics led her to make valuable contributions to the first (punchcard-activated) "computers" developed for the textile industry in the 1830s by Charles Babbage. For her part, Ada is generally regarded as the first computer programmer in world history.

REAR ADMIRAL GRACE HOPPER

Rear Admiral Grace Hopper

Known to her colleagues as "the first lady of software," Hopper was one of the inventors of COBOL, a milestone programming language. She was a brilliant mathematician who joined the Naval Reserve in 1943, where she helped to design the first large-scale digital computer, the Mark One, a breakthrough aid to ordnance calculations. She coined the phrase "computer bug" to describe errors in computer software function; when she retired from the Navy in 1986, she was the oldest active-duty military officer in the United States. She died in 1992 at the age of 85.

THE SURVIVORS
Women Who Looked Death in the Face and Lived to Tell the Tale

"Martha Martin" Her real name is unknown, but sometime in the middle 1920s this remarkable woman, used to summering in the Alaskan wilderness, was separated from her gold-prospecting husband after an unexpectedly severe storm. She was lucky to survive the subsequent avalanche near her camp, but lay pinned beneath the rocks for some days with a broken arm and a broken leg. Eventually she managed to extricate herself and use materials around the camp to approximate a splint and a cast. Tending her injuries was actually the least of her troubles: she was about seven months pregnant, and, as her attempts to return to civilization before the onset of winter failed repeatedly, she prepared to give birth on her own in the wilderness. Although she accomplished this, the child later died. "Martha," who had to hunt game to supplement her meager provisions, survived her ordeal and was eventually reunited with her husband. (He had been trapped some miles away.) The diary she had kept "to keep my sanity" was eventually sold for a tidy sum to a women's magazine under her assumed name.

Marie Dorion A member of the unlucky Astoria Expedition in 1811, Dorion was no tenderfoot. Pregnant, she rode twenty miles on horseback, gave birth to an infant son, and then walked twelve miles within a day of her delivery. (The baby died eight days later.) Not long after, her husband and a few other men in the group—separated from the main party—were massacred by Indians, and Marie set off into the wilderness with two small children, a horse, and the will to live. For nearly two months the family endured bonechilling blizzards, lived in a shaky hut constructed of branches, and ate twigs and berries (and, eventually, the horse). Dorion and both of her children survived the ordeal; they happened upon an Indian village that served as the first stop on the way to reunion with the main party.

MRS. MARGARET W. REED OF THE DONNER PARTY

Norma Hanson It's safe to say that no diver, male or female, has come out of a close encounter with a great white shark in quite the way Hanson did. Diving with her husband Al, off Catalina Island, Norma heard a distressing message from her partner over the headset: "Shark going for your legs!" Reacting from instinct and little else (she could not see the shark), she kicked powerfully with both legs. Her heavy steel boots went straight into the shark's open jaws— and sent dozens of teeth flying. The shark sped away, having met its match. Norma's commercial diving career went on unimpeded by her brush with disaster.

25 Female Members of the Donner Party Many are unaware of the remarkable survival rate of the women who set out on this ill-fated journey to California in 1846. Half the men perished, but twenty-five of the thirty-five women on the expedition survived the horrific winter in which eating the flesh of those who had perished was the only means of survival. California governor Peter Burnett had some theories on the anomaly, which was shown in even starker contrast in the survival rates of the members of the Forlorn Hope rescue party the starving emigrants sent out for help. Of that group, in which eight of the ten men perished but all five women survived, Burnett surmised that "taken altogether, the women performed more than the men; after the men had become too weak to carry the gun, it was carried by the women."

TEACH THE CHILDREN
Crossing New Horizons in Education

Margarethe Meyer Schurz

There are a number of claims for the site of the first kindergarten in the United States, but in actuality the historic spot is in Watertown, Wisconsin. It was in Watertown in the fall of 1856 that Margarethe Meyer Schurz, a student of the influential German infant education researcher Friedrich Froebel, first took neighbor children in and provided a controlled environment in which they could amuse themselves with colored blocks, balls, and other diversions. Schurz was the first in American history to foster creative play in a structured environment in this way as a means of getting preschoolers to "teach" themselves. ("Kindergarten" is German for "the children's garden.")

Lucy Laney

In 1886, Laney decided to devote her life to providing black children with a top-notch education. She started in a church basement, but within a few years she was overseeing a private school with over one thousand young black students. Among them was Mary McLeod Bethune, who would later become the nation's premier black educator. (See *Eleanor's Cabinet*, page 33.) Of Laney, McLeod (who had considered missionary work) would write, "From her I got a new vision: my life's work lay not in Africa, but in my own country."

Prudence Crandall

Crandall's female boarding school in Canterbury, Connecticut, operated quietly and with little notice until 1833, when a young black girl named Sarah Harris applied for admission. Crandall's decision to admit her set off a firestorm of controversy that resulted in mob attacks, the physical relocation of the class sites, and, eventually, Crandall's own imprisonment. The conflict was the turning point in the quiet Quaker woman's career; she decided to limit admission solely to young black women and vowed to work "the remaining part of my life to benefit the people of color."

MARGARETHE MEYER SCHURZ

THE THRONE AND THE SCEPTER
Female Monarchs Who Eclipsed
Their Royal Spouses

Hatshepsut Sometime circa 1500 B.C., Hatshepsut married her half-brother Thutmose II and became one of Egypt's major queens. When he died, she became Regent for the young Thutmose III; two years into that reign she became Pharaoh and the first woman to head the kingdom in two millennia. It is not entirely clear whether she eventually established a power-sharing arrangement with the young king or simply used him as a figurehead. What is known is that her reign was marked by energetic military campaigns in Nubia, a generally prosperous domestic period, and many cultural and architectural achievements. On her death, Thutmose III began a systematic campaign to erase her memory and discredit her rule. Her tomb in the Valley of the Kings was never completed.

Theodora Born in 497 A.D., she was an accomplished stage performer who developed numerous contacts within the Byzantine elite. Theodora became the mistress of a bureaucrat named Hecebolus and followed him in his travels through northern Africa; probably more influential on the development of her character were contacts with the patriarchs Timothy and Severus of Antioch. She returned to Constantinople, where she had grown up, and enchanted Justinian, who was heir to the throne. He changed existing law in order to marry a commoner and she became Empress in 527. She was one of the most powerful women in history, centuries ahead of her time—an activist female monarch who liberalized divorce and inheritage laws and tried to stamp out prostitution in the large cities. When she died of cancer in 548, Justinian was devastated. He accomplished little of consequence in the way of new laws during the rest of his reign.

Kaahumanu The favored wife of King Kamehameha I, Kaahumanu was one of Hawaii's most important transitional leaders, helping the island populace bridge the countless cultural gaps encountered in dealing with Western society around the turn of the century. Not infrequently, her nudges toward reform improved the quality of life for Hawaiian women. She broke a centuries-old taboo by eating in public with

TZ'U-HSI

Kamehameha I's son, and was responsible for introducing the first codified set of laws to the islands. (She was coruler with Queen Keopuolani.)

Tz'u-hsi Originally a concubine to the Emperor Hs'en Feng, she gained immense power in 1856 when she bore his only son. When the Emperor died in 1861, she became ruler of China in all but name; no decrees could stand without the Dowager Empress's seal of approval. She formed an alliance with the late Emperor's chief wife, Tz'uan. Tz'u-hsi handed the reins of power to others in 1889, then led a conservative coup following China's devastating defeat at the hands of the Japanese in the 1890s. She fled the capital during the Boxer Rebellion of 1900 but returned in 1901 to institute reforms she had once fought against. These included the prohibition of foot-binding, the legitimization of intermarriage between Chinese and Manchu, and the opening to girls of state educational facilities.

"THROUGH OUR EFFORTS, UNTO THE STARS"
Dramatic Stories of Commercial Success

Madame C.J. Walker
The world's first self-made female millionaire was Madame C.J. Walker (born Sarah Breedlove), and unschooled black orphan. She began her career as a door-to-door salesperson around the turn of the century, but later earned her fortune through the sale of cosmetics and the development of the Walker Method, a hair preparation process for African-American women. Madame Walker's zeal for cleanliness was legendary; many of her strict employee hygiene standards were incorporated into state and federal laws after her death.

Margaret Fogarty Rudkin
By 1937, Mrs. Margaret Rudkin had learned how to bake an excellent loaf of bread. She was so impressed by her results that she began to share her loaves with her Fairfield, Connecticut, neighbors. The reaction was so uniformly positive that she decided to try to place some of her goods in local stores. Thus began a home business that would become a multimillion-dollar concern, Pepperidge Farm, Inc. (Mrs. Rudkin named the firm after a beloved pepperidge tree in her home's front yard.) The firm's founding principle was its insistence on producing nothing but quality products, and that quality was due to Margaret Rudkin's careful, uncompromising approach to production.

Bette Clair Nesmith

Nesmith was the inventor of correction fluid. The company she founded on her Dallas, Texas, kitchen table to market the product eventually became a stationery-products giant: Liquid Paper Corporation. Nesmith, an executive secretary and working mother before she became president of the company that would make her rich, headed Liquid Paper until 1976. A subsidiary of her firm, L.P. Child Development Corporation, was opened to offer childcare to parents holding down full-time jobs.

MADAME C.J. WALKER

Carolina Maria de Jesus

A farmworker's daughter, Carolina was forced by her illiterate mother to go to school to learn how to read and write. After doing so, Carolina settled in Sao Paulo's slums, where she lived in a hovel and raised three children on her own. To feed them, she collected paper from the garbage on the streets and sold it to junkyards. As a means of temporary escape from her oppressive lifestyle, de Jesus wrote poems, plays, and stories. Her topics were broad-ranging: the rich, the countryside around her, and anything else that could help her forget about her surroundings. She also kept a diary about life in the slums; in it, she launched blistering attacks at Brazilian politicians, whom she considered responsible for the country's severe economic inequality. One day, her writing was discovered by a newspaper reporter visiting the slums who asked for—and received— permission to publish portions of her work. De Jesus's insights captivated the country, and her career was launched. Her diary was eventually published in book form; it became the best-selling title in Brazilian history.

TOUGH AS NAILS
Remarkable Accounts of
Physical Endurance

Jane Todd Crawford

She had been in agony for days with what was diagnosed as a massive ovarian tumor. The forty-seven-year-old Crawford, in severe pain, endured the sixty-mile horseback ride from Greensburg, Kentucky to the Danville offices of Dr. Ephraim McDowell. There she underwent a grueling, unanesthetized operation to remove the 22½-pound tumor. (The year was 1809, and painkillers had not yet been developed.) This was the first successful ovariotomy in medical history, and it marked a new era in abdominal surgery. Crawford was up and about less than a week later, making her own bed. She lived for thirty-three years after the landmark operation.

Kapiolani

This legendary Hawaiian high priestess, famous for her descent into the crater of Mount Kilauea and her leading role in the introduction of Christianity to the islands, was diagnosed with breast cancer later in life. As fearless in facing her illness as she was in facing the volcano, she underwent a radical mastectomy with no anesthesia—and survived.

Ruth Nichols

In June of 1931, this pioneering aviator broke five vertebrae and cracked up her airplane in an attempt to reach Paris from St. John, New Brunswick. She was told it would be impossible for her to fly again for at least one year, but three months later, wearing a steel corset that extended from her armpits to her hips, she mounted a successful attempt to break the existing world distance record by flying nonstop from Oakland, California, to New York City. She logged a landmark total of 1,977 nonstop miles in what could safely be called uncomfortable in-flight conditions.

KAPIOLANI

Mary Bacon

In 1974, horse jockey Mary Bacon was honored as the "Most Courageous Athlete of the Year," and it's no wonder. Her endurance has to rank as one of the most monumental achievements in sporting history. The list of injuries she sustained pursuing her sport include two broken backs and a broken collarbone; she was on hospital critical lists three times. These setbacks did not stop her from racing. As one of the top ten jockeys at Aqueduct, Bacon once rode in three consecutive races in one day. After the third and final race, she gave birth to her baby daughter.

TYCOONS
Female Business Successes

Hetty Green

This unpredictable, fabulously wealthy moneylender was so pathologically cheap that she refused to wash her clothes, stayed in flophouses with her two children, and once took her son, who had dislocated his knee, to a free clinic to avoid incurring hospital expenses. (She had waited too long before doing even that, and the lower part of her son's leg eventually had to be amputated.) Whatever her failings as a parent, Green was a financial genius who inherited more than $5 million upon the death of her parents and left her children over $125 million on her own passing in 1916. She survived innumerable panics on Wall Street, and usually found some way to profit from them. It was Green's ruthless approach to financial affairs that earned her notoriety as "the world's stingiest woman." If her compulsive ruthlessness led to remarkable stories of heartlessness toward her own family, however, they also beg the question, whether anyone would have looked askance at such personal problems had she been a man—and whether such a man might not have won fame, first and foremost, as a brilliant financier rather than a bitter, eccentric miser.

Maggie Lena Walker

A female, black bank president—in 1903 Virginia? Maggie Walker's story is truly an inspiring one. She abandoned a teaching position to study business and accounting and took a position as executive secretary and treasurer of a charitable organization. She was amazingly successful, turning the nearly destitute concern into a multimillion-dollar operation in a few years. In 1903, she took over management of Richmond's Consolidated Bank and Trust Company. The firm's name changed due to mergers over the years, but the hand at the rudder did not; she chaired the board until her death in 1934.

Mammy Pleasant

No one is quite sure exactly how much this eccentric nineteenth-century African-American boardinghouse operator was worth in her California heyday. Pleasant, who claimed to have financed John Brown's 1859 raid on Harper's Ferry, left a life of slavery in the South, practiced a variety of mystical rituals that carried

HETTY GREEN

significant public relations value, and became an influential and respected moneylender in San Francisco in the 1880s. She died in 1904.

UNDERCOVER IN BLUE AND GRAY
Spies in the Civil War

Pauline Cushman

Cushman performed invaluable Union spy work in 1863; she posed as an actress in search of her brother (purportedly in the Confederate army) to gather intelligence on rebel officers staying in a Shelbyville, Tennessee, hotel. She so enthralled one hapless captain that she was able to steal the drawings of defense fortifications he'd left lying about his room. These were then smuggled North. The Confederates eventually discovered her ruses and condemned her to hang, but Union forces rescued her before the sentence could be carried out. Cushman was eventually commissioned as a major in the federal army for her exploits.

Rose O'Neal Greenhow

She was one of Washington's most visible socialites when the war broke out, and she included in her social circle some of the most prominent figures in the Union leadership. She attempted to use her many social contacts to aid the Confederacy—and came up with a number of key successes. At least three messages from Greenhow reached Confederate officers; they were quite detailed, explaining exactly how many troops the rebels would face and when the attacks would take place. She was eventually discovered and imprisoned, but she was released to the Confederacy in 1862 on the condition that she stay out of Union territory. Confederate leader Jefferson Davis gave her a cash reward of $2500 upon her release.

Eugenia Phillips

Phillips was the subject of intense scrutiny by occupation Union offers, who had reason to suspect her of engaging in espionage activities for the South. When she made the mistake of laughing at a military funeral cortege passing her home in New Orleans in 1862, the authorities (who had been looking for a reason to take her out of commission) imprisoned the mother of nine. She was given rations considered unfit to serve other prisoners and confined to a tiny shack near a mosquito-infested bog. She endured her months of confinement stoically and eventually earned a measure of grudging respect from her captors.

ROSE O'NEAL GREENHOW

Elizabeth Van Lew

Around the Confederate capitol in Richmond, they called her "Crazy Bet," but there was a method to her madness. Van Lew cultivated the image of a harmless old eccentric; she was in fact a brilliant and passionate supporter of the Union cause who managed to plant an operative among Jefferson Davis's personal staff of servants. Her intelligence work was of incalculable aid to the Union assaults on Richmond and Petersburg in 1864 and 1865.

Belle Boyd

A notorious seductress and Confederate operative, "La Belle Rebelle" was arrested a half-dozen times for soliciting secrets from Union officers in Washington. She was banished from the North several times, and spent the latter part of the war abroad.

UNDER ENEMY FIRE
Creative Thinking that Helped the Cause

Prudence Wright
Shortly after the historic conflict at Lexington, Massachusetts in 1775 that was later termed "The Shot Heard Round the World," a group of women from the Massachusetts towns of Groton and Pepperell received word that a contingent of enemy troops and spies was heading southward from the Canadian border. Prudence Wright headed an assembly of women bearing muskets and pitchforks. Dressed in men's clothing, the group kept night watch at a local bridge and apprehended a British agent by the name of Leonard Whiting. Acting under the orders of "Captain Wright," the women found Whiting's orders from the Crown concealed in his boots and swiftly conveyed him to the authorities.

Rebecca and Abigail Bates
These young daughters of Scituate, Massachusetts's, lighthouse keeper are given credit for saving the town beacon from destruction during the War of 1812. An English man-of-war was poised to burn the lighthouse to the ground, but Rebecca and Abigail kept up such a huge racket with a fife and drum that the attackers, believing troops to be advancing on the position, sailed away.

Celia and Winnie Mae Murphree
These sisters were baby-sitting for friends in Blountsville, Alabama, in 1863 when

three Union soldiers stormed in demanding medical supplies and fresh horses. The soldiers took over the home and demanded to be served mint juleps. Celia and Winnie Mae dutifully prepared the drinks but mixed in a toothache medication that contained a powerful sedative. The Yankees loved the flavor of the drinks and ordered another round just like the first. They got it, drank deeply once again—and quickly passed out. The sisters took their weapons and turned the three in to a nearby Confederate camp.

ABIGAIL BATES

WEATHERING THE SEASONS
Women in the Midst of Political Upheaval

Marie Tussaud

From Bern, Switzerland, Marie and her widowed mother went to Paris in 1770 with Marie's brother Curtius, who was an accomplished wax-modeler with extensive connections in the French court. Marie developed her own skills as a modeler, and by 1780 was art tutor at Versailles to the French royal family. When the French Revolution occurred in 1789, the family scrambled to distance itself from the crown, but with limited success: Curtius was beheaded in 1794, and Marie was imprisoned. She was released in short order, however, and upon her release found herself the sole proprietor of her brother's waxworks. This she built into a phenomenon, and, once Marie had relocated to England, one of the most profitable entertainment concerns in Europe: Madame Tussaud's Waxworks. The prime attractions were death masks Marie herself had taken from the severed heads of French Revolution-era figures such as Marie Antoinette, Charlotte Corday, and Robespierre.

Alexandra Tolstoy

Helping her dying father, the legendary Russian writer Leo Tolstoy, escape from his wife and remaining children was but one of many unconventional acts of Alexandra Tolstoy's long and fascinating life. During the Russian Civil War, she allowed White Russians to gather in her home, a dangerous course of action which landed her in jail on numerous occasions. (That never stopped her from allowing the meetings upon her release.) She openly opposed the Soviet government, a risky proposition at best, and eventually tricked the government into letting her leave the country to which she would never return. When she arrived in the United States in 1931, she set up farms for elderly Russians and Russian immigrants and continued promoting her father's life and works.

Queen Liluokalani

QUEEN LILUOKALANI

Liliuokalini succeeded to the Hawaiian throne in 1891 upon the death of her brother. She was deeply loved by her people; her reign was marked by a concerted campaign to restore power to the Hawaiian monarchy and avoid annexation by the United States. These efforts were less than popular with the Hawaiian business community, which overthrew her in 1893, established a provisional government, and put her in jail for nine months. After her release, with the new government firmly in place, she was voted a pension and granted comfortable dwellings. She died in 1917.

WHAT HANDICAP?
Remarkable Women Who Overcame Great Physical Challenges

Laura Bridgman

Although Laura Bridgman survived the scarlet fever epidemic that killed her two sisters, the disease left her completely blind, deaf and mute, and destroyed much of Laura's sense of smell and taste. Between the ages of two and seven, Laura drifted beyond the world of human contact and stimulus. Upon hearing of her case, Dr. Samuel Gridley Howe, director of the Perkins Institute for the Blind in Watertown, Massachusetts, decided to challenge the popular belief that people like Laura could never be taught to communicate. Within a few months, Laura could write letters; within a few years she was writing poetry and, eventually, her autobiography. Bridgman later became an instructor at the Perkins Institute. Her successful case inspired Anne Sullivan, Helen Keller's "miracle worker."

Ada James

James was Wisconsin's most active suffragist, crisscrossing the state to win adherents to her cause. She was very nearly deaf, but this did not deter her from conducting her campaigns on behalf of the extension of the right to vote to women. James purchased the most sophisticated hearing aids available, turned them on during her speeches from the platform, and then disconnected them before her opponents had the chance to shout her down. It was an extremely effective rhetorical technique. Due largely to her tireless efforts, Wisconsin became the first state to ratify the Nineteenth Amendment, which gave women the right to vote nationwide.

Ruth Benedict

Deaf due to an early childhood illness and painfully shy, Benedict conducted countless hours of field research in foreign countries in quest of the underpinnings of human culture. She was one of anthropology's true pioneers; her work in the still-developing discipline included a series of remarkable studies of the patterns underlying cultural development. Dr. Benedict was a strong and influential proponent of the idea that cultures, rather than biological predisposition, are primarily responsible for the differences among the various races and nations of the world. In 1930, she became the first woman named to the anthropology faculty of Columbia University.

LAURA BRIDGMAN

WOMEN OF THE WEST
Memorable Figures from America's Frontier Days

Poker Alice

English-born Poker Alice became a gambling legend in the 1880s and 1890s. She and her first husband settled in Colorado and upon his death she was obliged to find some way to make a living. She settled on gambling, having observed hundreds of poker games while her husband was alive. Alice became one of the most legendary stud poker players in the West, and her lifetime winnings were estimated at half a million nineteenth-century dollars. She eventually opened up a gambling house of her own, complete with female companionship for male patrons. The authorities shut it down and put her in jail. After a discreet interval she received a pardon from the governor.

Ann Whitney

In 1867, schoolteacher Ann Whitney made a split-second decision that averted the cold-blooded slaughter of her pupils. During a Comanche raid on her tiny log cabin classroom, Whitney calmly led the students to an small open window where they escaped to safety; all the while, Whitney was shielding the children from the arrows entering the schoolhouse. Whitney herself was unable to escape through the window and died of multiple arrow wounds. In her memory and in thanks for her heroism, Whitney's students erected a memorial for her in the nearby cemetery.

Pamela Mann

In 1836, this Texas frontier woman entered into an agreement with legendary soldier and political figure Sam Houston: She lent him some oxen to transport two of his cannons. Houston agreed that the oxen would be used only so far as the town of Nacogdoches. Mann, suspicious that Houston might go back on his word, met him just past the town line brandishing "a pair of pistols and a long knife." She proceeded to call him (among other things) a liar, and, having finished the tongue-lashing, took back her oxen at gunpoint.

POKER ALICE

Elizabeth "Frenchy" McCormick

On their wedding day, dancing girl Elizabeth "Frenchy" McCormick and her gambler husband Mickey swore eternal fidelity to one other and promised never to leave their beloved town of Tascosa, Texas. Thirty-one years later, in 1912, Mickey died—but Elizabeth held fast to her vow. She stayed in Tascosa until her death in 1941, despite the fact that for twenty-four years she was the only citizen in town. Of course, her friends made sure Elizabeth was buried next to her husband.

"YOU CAN'T PLAY"
Women Who Fought for a Fair Chance—and Won!

Barbara Blount Hall

In 1804, Barbara Blount Hall had interests that went well beyond the abysmal educational prospects available to a young Southern female at the time. She took matters into her own hands and registered to study philosophy at the University of Tennessee. Her studies there earned Hall the title of "the nation's first coed" over eighty years before the official acceptance of women into the university, but there was a catch. Hall was not given the letter or point grades her male classmates received; she had to settle for benign adjectives like "diligent" to describe her progress in class.

Annie Baxter

Baxter was elected county clerk in Jasper County, Missouri, in 1890 but prohibited from serving on the grounds that it was illegal for women to hold office—any office—in Missouri. She went to court, and the case, which eventually reached Missouri's supreme court, was decided in her favor. She served for four years.

Ruth Bryan Owen (later Ruth Bryan Rohde)

Owen, daughter of legendary politician William Jennings Bryan, waged a grueling 10,000-mile campaign up and down the coast of Florida for the Fourth District congressional seat in 1928. When she won, she became the first woman ever elected to

Congress from the Deep South. Her opponents challenged her seat, however, by claiming that she had forfeited her American citizenship when she married a British subject (Reginald Owen, who had died a year before the election took place). Owen declined the funds she was entitled by law to use to hire a lawyer for her defense. Instead, she argued her case herself, won the right to represent her district, and focused national attention on the grossly inequitable state of U.S. independent citizenship and repatriation rights for women. (*Note:* This remarkable woman became the nation's first female diplomat when she was named head of the U.S. mission to Denmark by President Franklin D. Roosevelt in 1933.)

RUTH BRYAN OWEN

Kathy Switzer

Barred from running the Boston Marathon because of her gender, Kathy Switzer registered under her first initial for the 1967 race and showed up at the start line dressed in a full sweatsuit and hat to disguise her identity. During the race, officials realized she was a woman and attempted to stop her and rip the race number from her back. She made it to the finish line despite their efforts.

BIBLIOGRAPHY

Anderson, Bonnie S. and Judith P. Zinsser, *A History of Their Own, Volumes I and II*. New York: Harper & Row, 1988.

Brown, Dee. *The Gentle Tamers: Women of the Old Wild West*. Lincoln: University of Nebraska Press, 1958.

Canning, John, ed. *100 Great Kings, Queens and Rulers of the World*. New York: Bonanza Books, 1968.

Caroli, Betty Boyd. *First Ladies*. New York: Oxford University Press, 1987.

Cassutt, Michael. *Who's Who in Space: The First 25 Years*. Boston: G. K. Hall & Company, 1987.

Clark, Judith Freeman. *Almanac of American Women in the 20th Century*. New York: Prentice Hall Press, 1987.

Comay, Joan. *Who's Who in Jewish History-after the period of the Old Testament*. New York: David McKay Company, Inc., 1974.

Cooke, Alistair. *America*. New York: Alfred A. Knopf, 1974.

Culhane, John. *The American Circus: An Illustrated History*. New York: Henry Holt and Company Inc., 1990.

Diagram Group. *Mothers: 100 Mothers of the Famous and Infamous*. New York: Paddington Press, 1976.

Edward, James T., Janet Wilson James, and Paul S. Boyer, eds. *Notable American Women 1607-1950*. Cambridge, Massachusetts: Belknap Press, 1971.

Evans, Sara M. *Born For Liberty: A History of Women in America*. New York: The Free Press, 1989.

Felton, Bruce and Mark Fowler. *Felton & Fowler's Famous Americans You Never Knew Existed*. New York: Stein and Day, 1979.

Forbes, Malcolm and Jeff Bloch. *Women Who Made A Difference*. New York: Simon and Schuster, 1990.

Gilbert, Lynn and Gaylen Moore. *Particular Passions: Talks With Women Who Have Shaped Our Times*. New York: Clarkson N. Potter, Inc., 1981.

Grinstein, Louis S. and Paul J. Campbell, eds. *Women of Mathematics: A Biobibliographic Sourcebook*. New York: Greenwood Press, 1987.

Haight, Anne Lyon. *Banned Books: Informal Notes on Some Books Banned for Various Reasons at Various Times and in Various Places*. New York: R.R. Bowker Company, 1970.

James, Muriel. *Hearts on Fire: Romance and Achievement in the Lives of Great Women*. Los Angeles: Jeremy P. Tarcher, Inc., 1991.

Jezic, Diane Peacock. *Women Composers: The Lost Tradition Found*. New York: The Feminist Press, 1988.

Jordan, Teresa. *Cowgirls: Women of the American West*. Garden City, New York: Anchor Books, 1974.

Kane, Joseph Nathan. *Famous First Facts*. New York: The H.W. Wilson Company, 1981.

Kurzman, Dan. *The Bravest Battle: The Twenty-eight Days of the Warsaw Ghetto Uprising.* New York: G. P. Putnam's Sons, 1976.

Lamparski, Richard. *Whatever Became Of . . . ?* New York: Crown Publishers, Inc., 1970.

Macksey, Joan and Kenneth Macksey. *The Book of Women's Achievements.* New York: Stein and Day Publishers, 1975.

McCullough, David. *The Great Bridge.* New York: Simon and Schuster, 1972.

McHenry, Robert, ed. *Liberty's Women.* Springfield, Massachusetts: G. & C. Merriam Company, 1980.

McKay, John R., Bennett D. Hill, and John Buckler, eds. *History of Western Society, Volume I.* Boston: Houghton Mifflin Company, 1987.

Moffat, Mary Jane and Charlotte Painter, eds. *Revelations: Diaries of Women.* New York: Random House, 1974.

Moolman, Valerie. *Women Aloft.* Alexandria, Virginia: Time-Life Books, 1981.

Morgan, Robin, ed. *Sisterhood is Global: The International Women's Movement Anthology.* New York: Anchor Books, 1984.

Morison, Samuel Eliot. *The Oxford History of the American People, Volume II, 1789-1877.* New York: New American Library, 1965.

Morris, Richard B. *The Forging of the Union, 1781-1789.* New York: Harper & Row, Publishers, 1987.

Myron, Nancy and Charlotte Bunch, eds. *Women Remembered: A Collection of Biographies from the Furies.* Baltimore: Diana Press, 1974.

Nies, Judith. *Seven Women: Portraits from the American Radical Tradition*. New York: The Viking Press, 1977.

Olds, Elizabeth Fagg. *Women of the Four Winds*. Boston: Houghton Mifflin Company, 1985.

O'Neill, Lois Decker. *The Women's Book of World Records and Achievements*. Garden City, New York: Anchor Press, 1979.

Robertson, Patrick. *The Book of Firsts*. New York: Clarkson N. Potter, Inc., 1974.

Robbins, Trina and Catherine Yronwode. *Women and the Comics*. Forestville, California: Eclipse Books, 1985.

Sherr, Lynn and Jurate Kazickas. *The American Woman's Gazetteer*. New York: Bantam Books, 1976.

Sicherman, Barbara and Carol Hurd Green, eds. *Notable American Women: The Modern Period*. Cambridge, Massachusetts: 1980.

Sim, Kevin. *Women At War: Five Heroines Who Defied the Nazis and Survived*. New York: William Morrow and Company, 1982.

Smith, Carter, ed. *American Historical Images on File: The Black Experience*. New York: Media Projects, Incorporated, 1990.

Smith, Carter, ed. *American Historical Images on File: The Faces of America*. New York: Media Projects, Incorporated, 1988.

Smith, Gene. When The Cheering Stopped: The Last Years of Woodrow Wilson. New York: William Morrow and Company, 1964.

Sochen, June. *Herstory: A Women's View of American History*. New York: Alfred Publishing Co., Inc., 1974.

Uglow, Jennifer S., and Frances Hinton, eds. *The Continuum Dictionary of Women's Biography*. New York: Continuum, 1989.
—. *The International Dictionary of Women's Biography*. New York: Continuum, 1982.

Wallace, Amy, David Wallechinsky, and Irving Wallace. *The Book of Lists #3*. New York: Bantam Books, 1983.

Ward, Geoffrey C., Ric Burns and Ken Burns. *The Civil War*. New York: Alfred A. Knopf, Inc., 1990.

Wieser, Marjorie P. K. and Jean S. Arbeiter. *Womanlist.*, New York: Atheneum, 1981.

Zophy, Angela Howard and Frances M. Kavenik. *Handbook of American Women's History*. New York: Garland, 1990.

NEWSPAPERS
"Did Einstein's Wife Contribute to His Theories?" *New York Times*. Tuesday, March 27, 1990, p. C5.

MAGAZINES
Bennett, Dorothy. "Women Worthy of Honor: Maria L. Sanford." *DAR Magazine*. November 1991.

Caswell, Lucy Shelton. "Edwina Dumm: Pioneer Woman/Editorial Cartoonist, 1915-1917." *Journalism History 15:1*. Spring 1988.

Gordon, Mary Louise. "Belle Reynolds: That Remarkable Woman From Peoria." *DAR Magazine*. May 1991.

Youell, Mrs. Rice M, Jr., "Women Worthy of Honor: Caroline Lavina Scott Harrison." *DAR Magazine*. November 1990.
—. "Women Worthy of Honor: Julia Ward Howe." *DAR Magazine*. May 1991.
—. "Women Worthy of Honor: Ruth Bryan Owen Rohde." *DAR Magazine*. September 1991.
—. "Women Worthy of Honor: Dr. Kate Waller Barrett." *DAR Magazine*. June 1991.

MEDIA
National Public Radio, All Things Considered, January 3, 1992.

INDEX

Ludington, Sybil 58
Ludwig, King of Bavaria 80
Lukens, Rebecca Pennock 82-83
Lusk, Georgia 57
Lyon, Mary 104
Maconaqua (Frances Slocum) 86-87
Madison, Dolley 95
Mann, Pamela 137
Mansfield, Arabella Babb 71
Marge, (Marge Henderson Buell) 28
Maric, Mileva 50-51
Marshall, James 2-3
Martin, Martha 116
Maury, Antonia Caetana De Paiva Pereira 72-73
Mavrongenous, Manto 88
McCormick, Elizabeth "Frenchy" 137
McDowell, Dr. Ephraim 124
Menken, Adah Isaacs 80-81
Messick, Dale 29
Metoyer, Claude 82
Mitchell, Jackie 110
Mohammed 4
Monroe, Marilyn 65
Montagu, Lady Mary 12-13
Montez, Lola 80
Monvoisin, Catherine 46
Moody, Lady Deborah 40
Morgan, Julia 40-41
Morris, Esther Hobart 66
Mother Jones 90
Mozart, Amadeus 5

THE BOOK OF WOMEN

THIS IS ONLY THE BEGINNING!

Do you know of a woman whose story should be told? Send your suggestions along—they may become part of *The Book of Women II*. Write us at:

> *The Book of Women*
> c/o Bob Adams, Inc.
> 260 Center Street
> Holbrook, Massachusetts 02343

All entries become the exclusive property of Bob Adams, Inc.

ABOUT THE AUTHORS

Lynne Griffin grew up in southeastern Connecticut. She attended Providence College, where she graduated *magna cum laude* in history. She attended Blackfriar's College in Oxford, England. Ms. Griffin is currently a member of the editorial staff at Bob Adams, Inc., and is studying archaeology at Harvard University. She resides in Brookline, Massachusetts.

Kelly McCann grew up in the Lake George region of New York. She attended Brown University, where she earned a degree in music. Ms. McCann now lives in upstate New York, where she is working toward her master's degree in library science at the State University of New York at Albany.